Receiving 2 Thessalonians

Receiving 2 Thessalonians

*Theological Reception Aesthetics
from the Early Church to the Reformation*

ANDREW R. TALBERT

☙PICKWICK *Publications* • Eugene, Oregon

RECEIVING 2 THESSALONIANS
Theological Reception Aesthetics from the Early Church to the Reformation

Copyright © 2019 Andrew R. Talbert. All rights reserved. Except for brief quotations in critical publications or reviews, no part of this book may be reproduced in any manner without prior written permission from the publisher. Write: Permissions, Wipf and Stock Publishers, 199 W. 8th Ave., Suite 3, Eugene, OR 97401.

Pickwick Publications
An Imprint of Wipf and Stock Publishers
199 W. 8th Ave., Suite 3
Eugene, OR 97401

www.wipfandstock.com

PAPERBACK ISBN: 978-1-5326-7370-2
HARDCOVER ISBN: 978-1-5326-7371-9
EBOOK ISBN: 978-1-5326-7372-6

Cataloguing-in-Publication data:

Names: Talbert, Andrew R., author.

Title: Receiving 2 Thessalonians : theological reception aesthetics from the early church to the reformation / Andrew R. Talbert.

Description: Eugene, OR: Pickwick Publications, 2019 | Includes bibliographical references and index.

Identifiers: ISBN 978-1-5326-7370-2 (paperback) | ISBN 978-1-5326-7371-9 (hardcover) | ISBN 978-1-5326-7372-6 (ebook)

Subjects: LCSH: Bible. Thessalonians, 2nd—Commentaries—History. | Reader-response criticism. | Bible. Thessalonians, 2nd—Criticism, interpretation, etc.—History.

Classification: BS2725.2 T35 2019 (paperback) | BS2725.2 (ebook)

Manufactured in the U.S.A.   11/05/19

For Bethany
καλή μου

Contents

Acknowledgments | ix
Abbreviations | xi

1 Introduction | 1
2 The Early Church: John Chrysostom | 18
3 The Medieval Church: Haimo of Auxerre | 50
4 The Reformation: John Calvin | 81
5 Conclusion: Receiving 2 Thessalonians | 123

Bibliography | 129
Index of Subjects | 139

Acknowledgments

OVER THE YEARS I have composed quite a list of people who deserve acknowledgment for their various roles in helping to bring this work to fruition. And, despite some recent academic irritation with "acknowledgments," I intend to proceed with the custom.

This work began as a dissertation under Anthony Thiselton at the University of Nottingham, who took me on as his final doctoral student. His supervision and direction brought me to complementary nature of the work of H. R. Jauss and theological hermeneutics. As Anthony was edged into retirement, Richard Bell graciously supervised the remaining months of my dissertation and he was a sounding board for various ideas, both good and bad. As a German balance to these British scholars, my secondary supervisor and first reader, Roland Deines, brought together the theology postgraduates for presentations of our research, in which he systematically dismantled our arguments, structures, and sources. The remnants left in his wake were worth keeping, and the process made us better scholars. This supervisory balance was a great benefit to me.

My postgraduate and professional colleagues, who discussed ideas, offered feedback, read through my dissertation manuscript, and directed to further research, made this a work of interdisciplinary friendship of Aristotelian quality: Emily Gathergood, Eric Lee, Matthew Malcolm, Christoph Ochs, Peter Watts, and (as one untimely born) Seth Holler.

Several scholars aided me more than they know throughout the project: Mary Cunningham, for guidance on the Eastern Fathers; Wendy Mayer, for advice in reading John Chrysostom; Johannes Heil and Tom O'Loughlin, in regards to Haimo of Auxerre, and the former for sending me pre-publication material that helped immensely; Ormond Rush, who had the good fortune to study with Jauss and shared some of the insights he gleaned; John Milbank, who was patient and kind with emails from

Acknowledgments

a scholar on the biblical studies side of the theology-Bible divide; Murray Rae, for feedback and recommended revisions to bring the work to publication; Joel Green, who introduced me to theological interpretation and guided me in the proposal process that took me to Nottingham; and Christopher Rowland, my external reader, who gave critical feedback and directed me to Marxist literary theorists.

I owe a great deal of thanks to friends and family who supported us in Nottingham, especially John and Emily Gathergood, whose generosity made it possible for us to stay in the UK for an additional six months.

Of course, I am grateful to my mother and father, who have been a constant source of encouragement. To my now more immediate family, I thank my children for putting up with a father who disappears to read and write, and my wife, Bethany, who has encouraged, listened, advised, and moved all over the world with me.

Abbreviations

ANF	*Ante-Nicene Fathers*
ByzZ	*Byzantische Zeitschrift*
CO	John Calvin. *Ioannis Calvini opera quae supersunt omnia.*
CCCM	Corpus Christianorum: Continuatio Mediaevalis
CGPNT	*Catenae graecorum patrum in Novum Testamentum.*
CSEL	Corpus scriptorum ecclesiasticorum latinorum
CCSG	Corpus Christianorum: Series graeca.
CCSL	Corpus Christianorum: Series latina.
CTJ	*Calvin Theological Journal*
EuroJTh	*European Journal of Theology*
FC	Dressler, Hermigild, ed. *Fathers of the Church.*
FCT	*Ioannis Chrysostomi interpretatio omnium epistularum Paulinarum.*
HTR	*Harvard Theological Review*
IJST	*International Journal of Systematic Theology*
JEH	*Journal of Ecclesiastical History*
JSNT	*Journal for the Study of the New Testament*
LCL	Loeb Classical Library
LW	Luther, Martin. *Luther's Works.*
NICNT	New International Commentary on the New Testament
NIGTC	New International Greek Testament Commentary

ABBREVIATIONS

NovTSup	Novum Testamentum Supplements
NPNF1	*Nicene and Post-Nicene Fathers*, Series 1
NPNF2	*Nicene and Post-Nicene Fathers*, Series 2
OrChrAn	Orientalia Christiana Analecta
PG	*Patrologia Graeca*
PL	*Patrologia Latina*
RBén	*Revue Bénédictine*
RGG	*Religion in Geschichte und Gegenwart.*
SNTSMS	*Society for the Study of the New Testament Monograph Series*
ST	*Summa Theologiae*
StPatr	*Studia Patristica*
SVTP	Studia in Veteris Testamenti Pseudepigrapha
ThTo	*Theology Today*
WA	Luther, Martin. *D. Martin Luthers Werke.*
WTJ	*Westminster Theological Journal*
WUNT	*Wissenschaftliche Untersuchungen zum Neuen Testament*
ZNW	*Zeitschrift für die neutestamentliche Wissenschaft und die Kunde der älteren Kirche*

1

Introduction

> The Antichrist will go forth from the lower regions and the chasms of Hades. And he will come into a small garidion fish. And he is coming into the broad sea. And he will be caught by twelve fishermen. . . . He comes into Jerusalem and becomes a false teacher. And he will appear quiet and gentle and guileless. (*Apoc. of Dan.* 9:1–16)[1]

"Antichrist"—the malevolent herald of Christ's Second-Coming (and, incidentally, an enticing hook-word for beginning a book), but also a word of great importance that wends its way through the interpretation history of 2 Thessalonians. The inquiry into this figure has raised questions of great and ongoing ecclesiological import ("Do Calvin's or Luther's association of this figure with the papacy persist?"), the theologically mundane ("Will the Antichrist install his throne on the Mount of Olives?"), and even the typological oddity ("Will this Antichrist be circumcised?"). These parenthetical questions, and a great many more, are part of the nearly 2,000 year history of the aforementioned epistle, despite the fact that the term of interest does not even appear in 2 Thessalonians, let alone the Pauline corpus.

The book in progress charts the aesthetic-receptive history of 2 Thessalonians as it relates to the question-generative pressure of this letter and the broader hermeneutical frameworks within which these questions are put into play. With few exceptions in fundamentalism and broader

1. Charlesworth, *Old Testament Pseudepigrapha*, 1:767.

evangelicalism, hermeneutical scholarship has demonstrated the polyvalency of the Christian scriptures without a requisite Hirschian distinction between "significance" and "meaning"[2] or a devolution into the relativism of Nancian "sense."[3] Our project, then, is to consider a holistic hermeneutic that does justice to meaning-surplus *in, through,* and *with* history as it relates to the interpretation of 2 Thessalonians—a hermeneutic that does justice to biblical meaning both spatially and temporally. Such a holistic hermeneutic must simultaneously take seriously socio-historical contexts, theological trajectories, and the canonical form of scripture, but it must also exhibit a robustness that can place differing interpretations and methodological assumptions in dialogue while being a theological hermeneutic.

In many, if not in all of these ways, the literary-hermeneutical approach of *Rezeptionsästhetik* developed by Hans Robert Jauss provides precisely such an approach. Adopting and adapting this model, we seek not simply to record a history of interpretation of 2 Thessalonians, but to explore how particular actualisations, or concretisations, of the epistle have shaped the history of interpretation—so that the old continues to speak through the new[4]—and how the interpreters from various time periods unveil the truth-disclosive power of 2 Thessalonians in shifting contexts. "Reception" is taken over in this work as a theological category from the reader's perspective that corresponds to the divine acts of revelation and providence.

Rezeptionsästhetik is a summons to remain open to the content and claims of the text, to perceive the questions that the text and interpretations open for later generations, and to recognize the reader's role in meaning-production. These aims are a sharpening of the proposals mentioned above. As the hermeneutical framework of this project, *Rezeptionsästhetik* receives more detailed attention in due time.

Though the bulk of this work concentrates on the interpretation of 2 Thessalonians during discrete historical occasions, it would be insufficient to explore these actualisations without first articulating several critical issues and a methodology that propel this project. Additionally, the scope of this work requires a *selection* of pre-modern representatives. Therefore, the figures that follow have been selected from general periods of church

---

2. Hirsch, *Validity in Interpretation*, 1–23; Osborne, *Hermeneutical Spiral*, 21–23. Or even the retreat to "authorial intention." See Bockmuehl, "Commentator's Approach," 57.

3. Nancy, *Sense of the World*.

4. Jauss, "Tradition, Innovation, and Aesthetic Experience," 375.

INTRODUCTION

history to demonstrate influential perspectives from their respective eras, and to situate them in the exegetical contexts in which they arose through dialogue with contemporaries: John Chrysostom, Haimo of Auxerre, and John Calvin. The selection of these three readers of 2 Thessalonians has to do with their place in its history as "epochal" interpreters. That is, they have exerted significant influence in the reception history of 2 Thessalonians, including on each other.

The first chapter concentrates on *Rezeptionsästhetik* and the idea of "reception" as a theological category for a program to explore the historical receptions of a text and as a model that provokes any actualisation of a text with the expected, positive outcome of expanding one's horizon of understanding. In so doing, *Rezeptionsästhetik* illuminates the continuity between the historical eras of biblical interpretation, foregrounds exegetical conclusions reached in the history of interpreting 2 Thessalonians, and considers the roles that time, place, and culture play in a theology of reception and revelation.

The three chapters that follow engage with pre-modern exegetes in a pattern that attempts to disclose the "aesthetic value"[5] of their readings in their "horizon of expectation"[6] through dialogue with their contemporaries. Therefore, chapter 2 introduces John Chrysostom—the primary example of patristic interpretation of 2 Thessalonians. In this chapter, we explore a number of his interpretive assumptions (e.g., biblical inspiration and canon) as well as his exegetical decisions in both his homilies on 2 Thessalonians and other texts in which he incorporates the epistle.

Haimo of Auxerre represents a medieval voice in chapter 3. His brief commentary on the epistle became a standard of interpretation in the generations that followed, and his ability to blend patristic thought with his own insights make his work an "epochal" moment in the history of 2 Thessalonians. The combination of the fact that few modern biblical scholars are familiar with his work and his perspective as a monk at the height of the Carolingian era who asks historically-shaped questions of this biblical book provides a provocative engagement with modern horizons of expectations as they relate to 2 Thessalonians.

---

5. Jauss, *Toward an Aesthetic*, 25.

6. This is the crux of Jauss's third and fourth theses (discussed below) and much of his methodology. See Jauss, *Toward an Aesthetic*, 25–32; *Question and Answer*, 224–26; Parris, *Reception Theory*, 148–52.

By the Reformation, we turn to the work of the man of Picardy, John Calvin, on 2 Thessalonians. This includes a discussion on his historically-effected reading of the epistle, as well as an exploration into how Calvin interprets 2 Thessalonians in *The Institutes*, his commentary on the letter, and other theological works.

The concluding chapter remarks on the importance of reception history for biblical studies and the insights that the respective scholars bring to the interpretation of 2 Thessalonians specifically and scripture more generally. A theologically-oriented reception history, which we propose, extends the challenge against historical-positivist hermeneutics as the *primary* framework deployed to elicit biblical meaning[7] and it offers an advantageous hermeneutical model more in tune with the liturgical interests of scripture.

WHY 2 THESSALONIANS?

Before proceeding on the topic of reception history, we must address two preliminary questions. First, why 2 Thessalonians? There are several parts to this answer. Most notably, the size of the epistle enables us to examine the reception history of the entire letter and therefore to construct a fuller picture of the paradigm within which it is understood. Secondly, 2 Thess 2:1–12 has a rich history of interpretation, and is thus primed as a case study for our hermeneutical endeavor. Thirdly, and related to the previous point, the very nature of apocalyptic literature, like 2 Thessalonians, results in a referential openness that allows for ongoing appropriation and reinterpretation.[8] Further to this, 2 Thessalonians briskly sweeps through a variety of theological loci within an eschatological vision: ecclesiology (especially church discipline), anthropology (the suffering and victorious Christian), hamartiology (the ongoing and future effects of sin), and "last things"—all of which are secured in the Christ-event and cast the reader's gaze forward. So much transpires in such a brief space that touches on perennial human experiences and it invites ongoing interaction as time marches on toward

---

7. As Evans has shown, Gadamer and Jauss do not offer an either-or approach, but they see historical-critical methods as incorporated within the project of reception history, and not as something that must abandoned. See Evans, *Reception History*, 26–52.

8. Taking Antichrist as his sample figure, Hughes speaks of him as "a symbol that 'gives rise to thought' along several different vectors, and his meaning is not exhausted in any one interpretation" (Hughes, *Constructing Antichrist*, 6–7).

its consummation. Lastly, the apocalyptic eschatology of 2 Thessalonians appropriately orients attention to the "subject matter" of scripture and the world that the scriptures project.[9]

PSEUDONYMITY

The second question has to with the dubious authorship of 2 Thessalonians. This challenge does not affect *Rezeptionsästhetik*, per se, though it certainly engenders issues related to divine speech, meaning, and authority. Engaging with the weighty arguments of Wrede and Trilling against the authenticity of 2 Thessalonians detracts from the overall aim of this project.[10] This work proceeds with the assumption of Pauline authorship of the epistle—and uses such language—primarily on the grounds of the early Church's overwhelmingly negative view and *reception* of pseudonymous literature,[11] the linguistic relationship of the epistle to the broader Jewish (particularly Qumran) and Christian literary contexts, and stylometric comparisons with the other epistles of the Pauline corpus.[12] The debate over this issue is for another place and time.

SCRIPTURE

In addition to the questions above, it is worth clarifying one semantic cluster at the outset that has been hinted at in the preceding material: the terms "Bible," "scripture," and "word of God" feature somewhat interchangeably throughout this work. "Authority" is a helpful term for formulating a working definition of the Bible as Christian "scripture" that must be worked out in two directions.

In one direction, speaking of the Bible as scripture, or more pointedly as "the word of God," bespeaks the assumed authority that gives certain

9. i.e., God revealed through the eschatological consummation of history in Jesus Christ and history taken up in the salvific purposes of the Divine economy. See Beker, *Paul the Apostle*, 11, 20.

10. These two scholars offer the most substantial cases against the Pauline authorship of 2 Thessalonians, over against marginal figures like Schmidt, Kern, Holtzmann, Baur, Masson, and Marxsen.

11. For significant defenses of this position, see Baum, *Pseudepigraphie*; Wilder, *Pseudonymity*.

12. Mealand, "Extent of the Pauline Corpus"; Foster, "Who Wrote 2 Thessalonians?," 164.

biblical speech-acts their currency. For example, the pronouncement of "grace and peace" (2 Thess 1:2), or Paul's command that his readers avoid idleness (3:6–12)—both of which constitute illocutionary exercitive speech-acts—or promissory texts (e.g., "the Lord is faithful. He will establish you and guard you against the evil one," 3:3)[13] that have the aim of making the extra-textual world (including the assumed "spiritual world") match the words of promise;[14] the Triune God stands behind such speech-acts. Scripture is authoritative because it participates in God's authority.[15] The same holds true for blessings, charges, hallowing, condemning, etc. In reading the Bible, the reader is addressed, regardless of whether they accept or agree with its content. In this sense, the Christian scriptures are regarded as authoritative as the written word, even as it sits on a table or bookshelf, because it *contains* Divine speech-acts.

This naturally raises questions about addressees and whether letters or books written in/for particular historical communities have the same force for later readers. That is to say, are modern readers of scripture addressed directly? On this point, we head in that second direction on the topic of authority, namely that Christian scripture derives its authority from its character as witness to the (immanent) Triune God revealed in Jesus Christ—the proleptic consummation of history in the salvific economy of the Godhead. Not to be conflated with the revelation itself, scripture's proximity to and quality of orienting believers to Christ render it the Church's highest authority. Consequently, insofar as scripture participates in God's authority through his self-revelation, it is authoritative.[16] In this way, scripture becomes the medium provided by God *within the (ontological) space provided* for God's ongoing self-revelation for the purpose of salvation. Numerous scriptures might be enlisted to support a view of the Bible as the locus of ongoing Divine speech (2 Tim 3:16; Heb 1:2; 4:7, 12), but unless this analogical activity is also lucidly linked up with a clear sense of biblical authority, including the gift of ontological space, the Church risks a form of "pneumatological deism."[17]

Yes, as people continue to read scripture in the ontological gift of reality, God speaks through his word for His salvific purposes, and this is

---

13. All scripture quotations are taken from the ESV unless otherwise noted.
14. Thiselton, *New Horizons*, 283–301.
15. Paddison, "Authority of Scripture," 455.
16. Paddison, "Authority of Scripture," 455–57.
17. Wannenwetsch, "Conversing with the Saints," 132.

particularly the case when scripture is read appropriately (i.e., liturgically), because the readers are properly oriented toward the Speaker and Subject Matter of scripture.[18] And these historical hearings of the witness to revelation are truly in-*spired* insofar as they are the outgoing work of the Spirit that draws readers into the economy of the Godhead. After all, "Whoever has an ear, let him hear what the Spirit *says* to the churches" (Rev 2:7, 11, 17, 29; 3:6, 13, 22).[19]

These topics of biblical authority and inspiration connect directly with the larger interest of this particular book in that reception history charts and considers the inspired, revelatory, salvific work of God through scripture and history in various socio-cultural circumstances. Though it must do so cautiously and with a robust theology of providence,[20] while also bearing in mind the historical abuse of the Bible for various ends.

Having defined the contours of these terms, we turn now to another keyword: *Rezeptionsästhetik*. What follows is an overview of this concept and its potential import of this hermeneutics into biblical interpretation.

RECEPTION AESTHETICS AND THEOLOGICAL AESTHETICS

In the field of hermeneutics, Hans-Robert Jauss (1921–1997) proposes two unique ideas that might encapsulate his work: *aesthetics* as the starting point for hermeneutics, and *aesthetics* understood primarily under the concept of *reception*. His neologism, *Rezeptionsästhetik*, wed these two terms so as to foreground the role of the recipient and the societal function of art.[21] This prioritization of aesthetics proceeds from the simple observation that readers understand and enjoy historically-distant literature without

---

18. Recall Thomas Aquinas: "The act of faith is ultimately directed towards what is expressed, not the formula itself in which it is expressed" (Thomas Aquinas, *ST* 2.1.2.2).

19. Rae connects these two directions of biblical authority in insisting that speaking of scripture as "an instrument of divine communication is to say that scripture has a role in the saving economy of the Father, the Son, and the Holy Spirit. Scripture bears witness to the actions of God through which a people is called, established, nurtured, and equipped to be an instrument and embodied anticipation of the coming kingdom of God" (Rae, "Biblical Theology," 143).

20. Elliott does precisely this in his twin-volumes on providece. See Elliott, *Heart of Biblical Theology*; *Providence Perceived*.

21. Rush, *Reception of Doctrine*, 67.

first knowing the historical contexts in which it arose. The *primary* hermeneutical bridge for readers is aesthetic rather than historical.

The influence of Gadamer's thought from Jauss's time at Heidelberg is evident in his conceptual procession along the *via Gadamer*: preconceptions, tradition, history, horizons, dialogue, understanding, meaning, and aesthetics frame the lineaments of Jauss's method. Yet, that very word, "method," already indicates his divergence from Gadamer, which Jauss expands in several directions in his inaugural lecture at the University of Konstanz, *Literaturgeschichte als Provokation der Literaturwissenschaft*. This lecture introduced the collective proposal of university's literary studies program that came to be known as "reception history." Additional Marxist influences (in which Jauss recognized the formative power of literature on society and its dialectal relationship to other texts and readers,[22] while being cautious of tradition) and formalist influences (which contributed to his diachronic and synchronic understanding of literature) ultimately aided Jauss in foregrounding the role of the reader in the life of a text and meaning-production.[23]

Jauss draws on these resources while also moving beyond them, an accomplishment reached in part by understanding literature as a "triangle" consisting of author, work, and the public, the last of which is a historically-constructive energy[24] and the one for whom the work is primarily written; readers are co-creators of meaning, or, put differently, meanings do not merely subsist in a text, but are generated in the act of reading.[25] Texts do not lifelessly yield their singular meaning to communities over the generations, but "*texts have a formative influence upon readers and society*" and "*changing situations also have effects on how texts are read.*"[26] From this base

---

22. Jauss, *Toward an Aesthetic*, 14–16. This direction, as well as the influence of Heidegger is immediately evident in the opening paragraph of Kosík's work, in which he speaks of dialectical thinking as human praxis by which "man approaches reality primarily and immediately not as an abstract cognitive subject . . . but rather as an objectively and practically acting being, an historical individual who conducts his practical activity related to nature and to other people and realizes his own ends and interests within a particular complex of social relationships" (Kosík, *Dialectics*, 1). Kosík in particular breaks from the mimetic aesthetics of Marxists like Lukács in arguing that, rather than perpetuating an aesthetics of abstraction, "the work lives to the extent that it has influence" (Kosík quoted in Jauss, *Toward an Aesthetic*, 15).

23. Jauss, *Toward an Aesthetic*, 16.

24. Jauss, "Literaturgeschichte," 127.

25. Iser, *Prospecting*, 5.

26. Thiselton, *Hermeneutics of Doctrine*, 99.

INTRODUCTION

of influences, Jauss proposes *Rezeptionsästhetik,* which he establishes in seven decisive theses described as a methodological grounding of literary history.[27]

Rezeptionsästhetik: Seven Theses

The first thesis rejects historical objectivism's specious freedom from influences and underscores "the role of the reader as the thread connecting a literary history of works. Because a work comes to effect in the response of the reader, the history of the work is to be conceived like a dialogue arising out of the horizon of expectation of the producer, work and readers in different historical periods of the work's reception."[28] Literary history perceives this dialogue of the given text's history and gauges its aesthetic value by the "rightness" of the question that it poses with reference to the subject matter of the text and in relation to the original work and interpretations thereof. The ongoing reception of a text is then the progressive witness to the "beautiful" that coincides with the unfolding of truth. Jauss counters historical positivism with "aesthetics" as a study of the "beautiful" as it appears in the reception of a text through history, with particular emphasis on its evocative, communicative, and formative aspects (i.e., the cognitive experience of the reader).[29] When Jauss speaks of "aesthetic pleasure" he has in mind the immediate accessibility a reader has to otherness of a text via the pleasure of reading that is constitutive of understanding. It is "an interplay of subject and aesthetic object in which there is pleasurable enjoyment of oneself in the encounter, as well as a pleasurable focus on the object that frees the knower from the constraints of everyday existence."[30] In this approach, the reader first commits his/herself to the direction of the text and takes on its perspective, because "aesthetic pleasure does not need the bridge of historical knowledge"[31] in order to experience the text.

27. Jauss, *Toward an Aesthetic,* 20.
28. Rush, *Reception of Doctrine,* 40.
29. This definition of "aesthetics" Jauss formulates against the conceptions of aesthetics in "the objectivism of historical positivism, the essentialism of all substantialist notions of art, and any notion of art for art's sake alone" (Rush, *Reception of Doctrine,* 65). Significantly, "art" is not the object, but the triadic interrelation of author, work, and receiver as an "ongoing event of communication" (Rush, *Reception of Doctrine,* 71).
30. Rush, *Reception of Doctrine,* 49.
31. Rush, *Reception of Doctrine,* 16.

This response, which is a cognitive act gauged in terms of pleasure, marks the foundation of what Jauss terms the "aesthetic experience." It is an "aesthetic" experience because it is an orientation to the reader's experience of the work. This provides a provisional understanding of "aesthetic" in Jauss's work.[32]

In his second thesis, this model of reception history prioritizes the reconstruction of the "horizon of expectations" as an "objectifiable system of expectations that arises for each work in the historical moment of its appearance,"[33] and it includes the horizons of later receptions. Three elements constitute this horizon: familiarity/expectations with regard to the genre of a work, intertextual relationships, and the relationship of the world created by the text and the reader's world.

Thirdly, the tradition-transmitting qualities, the socially-formative function,[34] and the ways in which a work "satisfies, surpasses, disappoints, or refutes" the horizon of expectations of readers "provides a criterion for the determination of its aesthetic value."[35] Regarding the category of negation/provocation, an aesthetically distant[36] text can radically transform a reader's horizons. This "aesthetic distance," however, disappears over the generations, and therefore requires later readers to reconstruct the original horizon of its appearance (thesis two) in order to best appreciate its aesthetic value.

The fourth thesis introduces the concept of dialogue: readers both rediscover the historical questions to which the text was an answer, but they also pose their own questions to and receive answers from the text. The horizons of the past do not replace the present reader's horizon of expectation. Instead, they create a potential for the "change" of the present horizon, marked by an expansion in depth of the reader's understanding.[37]

---

32. Several scholars have summarized Jauss's theses well while also drawing out implications for biblical studies and doctrine. See Evans, *Reception History*, 10–13; Parris, *Reception Theory*, 129–47; Rush, *Reception of Doctrine*; Thiselton, *Hermeneutics*, 317–19. Our path seeks to baptize his method in theological aesthetics.

33. Jauss, *Toward an Aesthetic*, 22.

34. These two qualities account for the perseverance of classic texts. See Jauss, *Question and Answer*, 224–25; Parris, *Reception Theory*, 137–38.

35. Jauss, *Toward an Aesthetic*, 25.

36. "Distance" is gauged according to a work's deviation from the horizon of expectations of the original audience.

37. Jauss, "Alterity and Modernity," 182. Understanding is, according to Jauss, dialogical in nature.

Though Jauss elevates the answering nature of texts as the primary point of reception,[38] he views answers as belonging to the same horizon as questions, not preceding them.[39]

In the fifth thesis, Jauss proposes a diachronic examination of a text, which reveals how it confronted the horizon of expectations at the time of its appearance by disclosing the questions left behind by previous works to which the new work sought an answer.

Complementing diachrony, an aesthetics of reception views literary history in terms of synchrony, thereby revealing the changes in interpretation that have occurred over time. By looking at a moment in history during a text's reception, the reader can see the forms, influences, genres, and contemporary works of a particular reception, which illuminate particular "epoch-making" moments in the reception of a text.[40]

The final thesis advocates lived praxis in terms of the "socially formative function of literary texts,"[41] which is a "genuine possibility only where the literary experience of the reader enters into the horizon of expectations of his lived praxis, preforms his understanding of the world, and thereby also has an effect on his social behavior."[42]

These theses describe the general method of *Rezeptionsästhetik*, and might be summarized in Jauss's adaptation of three Aristotelian categories for the aesthetic experience of reading texts: *poiesis*—an aesthetically perceptual level of reading, which makes possible the concretization of meaning in the construction of the aesthetic object; *aesthesis*—a retrospectively interpretive level, which includes the reconstruction of the original horizon of expectations, but also considers particular concretisations of meaning throughout the text's history; and *catharsis*—a formative level of reading.[43]

---

38. Jauss, *Toward an Aesthetic*, 69.

39. This he offers in response to Pannenberg's contention for the precedence of the question in dialogical understanding. Pannenberg, *Basic Questions*, 1:123–28.

40. Thiselton, *Hermeneutics*, 318.

41. Thiselton, *Hermeneutics of Doctrine*, 100.

42. Jauss, *Toward an Aesthetic*, 39. Though Jauss is hesitant to connect with regional hermeneutics, here we recognize the interplay with theological aesthetics—"Only if the form of Christ can be lived out in the community of the church, is the confession of the church true; only if Christ can be practiced is Jesus Lord" (Hart, *Beauty of the Infinite*, 1).

43. Jauss, *Toward an Aesthetic*, 139. Though the steps pass through varying emphases on the reader, author, and text, above all this method draws out the importance of the reader in Jauss's method. Rush, *Reception of Doctrine*, 115.

Jauss also approaches texts from the direction of a comprehending consciousness that participates in the aesthetic experience of the "other." His method expands the aesthetic experience of a text, by drawing the reader from their initial aesthetic response through the historical otherness of the text and mediating the original aesthetic experience of the text.[44] This passage through the fullness of a text's alterity leads to a reader's deeper self-understanding through the appropriation of historically-distant questions, which can have a formative effect on the reader, and it concludes the aesthetic experience. The aesthetic experience is both pre-reflective, in that it is initially composed of a reader's pleasurable reading of a text, and reflective, because of the critical work of reconstructing historical horizons and the formulation of meaning as a response to reading.[45] Therefore, aesthetic experience is the *cognitive pleasure* of a reader as they understand, interpret, and apply a text.

The key advantage of *Rezeptionsästhetik* is that it provides *a method* for gauging the aesthetic quality of texts over against essentialist aesthetics, or the excavatory aesthetics of positivism that does not also integrate the progressive historical dimension of a text, which constitutes its "being." It also makes readers more aware of the historicality of their interpretations and of those past, aiding in the consideration of the appropriateness of their reading with regard to the subject matter of the text. With regard to readers in particular, the emphasis on aesthetic experience wrests control of biblical texts from specialists and elevates the place of the average, educated reader and the Christian community, for whom such texts were written.

From a theological perspective, however, aesthetics apart from the True and the Good inevitably falters. Revelation and the Real must qualify the beautiful; or rather aesthetics must be seen "as a measure of what theology may call true."[46] By way of example, if Jauss's category of "aesthetic value" is simply comparative in nature, then it must also speak of the "beauty" of Nietzsche's Übermensch as received in the manifestos of serial killers.[47]

---

44. Hart's contention that beauty is the true form of distance resounds here. "Beauty inhabits, belongs to, and possesses distance, but more than that, it gives distance . . . beauty is the showing of what is" (Hart, *Beauty of the Infinite*, 18). Aesthetic pleasure must be more ontologically grounded than Jauss is able to do apart from theology.

45. Parris, *Reception Theory*, 168–89.

46. Hart, *Beauty of the Infinite*, 3. Or, as Elliott notes, "Literature untied from theological questions is often prone to be interpreted in a lop-sided way" (Elliott, *Heart of Biblical Theology*, 67).

47. Bavinck observes, somewhat more elegantly, "Is it only the form that counts . . .

Introduction

Thus, the ongoing reception of a text is not the progressive unfolding of truth, as described in his first thesis, but simply the ongoing reception of the text. Further questions for *Rezeptionsästhetik* as an appropriate tool for biblical interpretation include: how does this method work with biblical "works," which claim themselves to be authoritative and revelatory, as do the orthodox Christian communities? Does this method so prioritize the reader that it actually excludes the revelatory event that produces faith and is central to Christian doctrine? Below we offer an attempt to recapture "reception" as a theological category with insinuations about the potential union between *Rezeptionsästhetik* and theological aesthetics.

"Reception" as a Theological Category

Ormond Rush draws several connections between *Rezeptionsästhetik* and the hermeneutics of doctrine, making "Christian joy" corollary to aesthetic pleasure and the appropriateness of "reception" over the idea of doctrinal "development." Most significantly, Rush qualifies *Rezeptionsästhetik* for the reception of Church doctrine "on account of the claim of revelation and the authority of Scripture." Regarding the former, he appeals to the "'historicity of the mediation of truth,' which in turn is grounded on the historicity of the supremely revelatory Christ-event. As revelation in Christ is itself not understood as a supra-historical event, rather as an event embedded in time and culture, so also is apprehended each conciliar decision of a determined epoch of understanding and proclaiming the truth, without the truth thereby being relativized."[48] He even goes so far as to suggest that reception "could provide the structuring principle for a whole systematic theology, with reception aesthetics and hermeneutics providing its investigative principle,"[49] because of how it captures human reception of God's self-communication in the gift of Christ, which affects all of Christian praxis.

Though Rush concentrates on the reception of Catholic doctrine, his work naturally extends to the reception of scripture in a variety of media that, though not doctrinal, are influential moments in reception history

---

or is beauty essentially bound to content, as well as to truth and goodness, and even if it were possible, is it really permissible to break this triad? In short, is Satan beautiful if he appears as an angel of light?" (Bavinck, "Of Beauty and Aesthetics," 257).

48. Rush, *Reception of Doctrine*, 167.
49. Rush, *Reception of Doctrine*, 167.

and/or attempts at faithful, focused articulations of the apostolic kerygma. That is to say, the dogmas are summaries, while the occasions of receiving particular biblical books are unabridged compliments to said dogmas. For a theology of reception, Rush clarifies how Jauss's concepts of "the work of art" and "the receiver" should be translated into theological analogues by considering the object/s of theological reception and the recipients of this object.

Rush proposes four objects of reception that are part of an intersecting process leading to the formulation and practice of doctrine: the Word of God, scripture, tradition, and doctrinal statements. Different from literature, what the Christian community receives first in biblical reception is the Word of God—God's self-communication, the content of revelation through Christ in the Spirit, which continues to happen within history.[50] This object begins already to explain the second. "Scripture constitutes the primary norm among the witnesses to revelation and its reception . . . the scriptural testimonies are themselves receptions of the Word."[51]

The third object, the living tradition, "signifies the norm, the environment, the means, the process and the content of the transmission of faith. The norm is the apostolic tradition; the environment is the church; the means are worship, Christian life and doctrine; the process is rejuvenating reception; and the content is the witness through the word and deed to the mystery of Jesus Christ, the Word."[52] This object is the particular interest of biblical reception history, which looks at normative and influential interpretations for the purpose of guiding and "rejuvenating" present interpretations.

Doctrinal statements, the fourth object, also relate to the reception of scripture, in that these statements provide guidelines or measures for acts of interpretation. Christian receivers of scripture naturally hesitate to interpret the book in any way that might contravene ecumenical doctrines. The fact that they do so points to the important role played by the receiving community, which must also be fleshed out in theological terms.

Though Rush details twelve, mutually receptive relationships, let us describe the receiver (whether individual or communal) as the "mediator of the revelatory process." With this definition of "receiver," reception history of the Bible looks at moments in which the Word of God was received,

---

50. Rush, *Reception of Doctrine*, 180–82.
51. Rush, *Reception of Doctrine*, 184.
52. Rush, *Reception of Doctrine*, 187.

INTRODUCTION

denied, or corrupted, and gauged by its aesthetic value in relation to the four objects of reception. It considers both that revelation requires a receiver and, in moments of faithfulness to the Word, the doctrine of providence has been realized.

By way of summary, we should draw out several benefits of a theologically-deployed *Rezeptionsästhetik*. Generally speaking, it recaptures the delight of reading old texts. More specifically, it aids in the rediscovery of older approaches to reading scripture, especially the implied ontology and epistemology of these readings, most notably an understanding of "truth" as "being" that characterizes pre-modern authors' horizons, over against the modern tendency to identify "truth" with "fact."[53] In this discovery, as well as the particular emphases of other interpreters, other readings provoke our horizons of understanding and, conversely, it allows for the readers' to contribute to the texts meaning from their contexts, while still subjecting their understanding to scrutiny. Lastly, *Rezeptionsästhetik* is "naturally" open to interdisciplinary collaboration and insights because of the centrality of beauty (as well as readers and history) to the method, rather than the ideology of positivism.

Yet, Candler takes Jauss and Rush further in recognizing the diachronic and synchronic "meaning" of scripture, because it "reaches across the historical life of the body of Christ and looks forward to the eschatological fulfilment of that meaning, and it makes sense within the liturgy of the Church as it is performed daily."[54] Such reading is performed within the entire historical body of Christ like an enormous, trans-temporal glossed Bible. But Candler also pushes Jauss's seventh thesis in a "meaning-ful" (that is *teleological*) way by noting "the practice of reading . . . is the 'art' of conforming one's will to the likeness of Christ, by virtue of the 'baptism' of understanding, which is transformed into wisdom, indeed the very wisdom of God himself, the Son of God. Thus the soul is drawn into fuller participation in the mystery of the Trinity."[55] Reading within the Christian community orients human desire to its proper referent: God. Theological *Rezeptionsästhetik*, therefore, leads to the possession of more "being," to

---

53. Ratzinger, *Introduction to Christianity*, 57–69.
54. Candler, *Theology, Rhetoric, Manuduction*, 77.
55. Candler, *Theology, Rhetoric, Manuduction*, 51.

becoming more truly human,[56] by enabling the "form of Christ"[57] to be inhabited, rather than simply "preforming" one's understanding of the world and affecting their behavior.

Using terms like "truth," "meaning," and "beauty" in a such a definite sense should make clear that we proceed under a form of Christian realism that acknowledges revelation, and that this sharpens the aesthetic dimension of Jauss's program because:

> The Christian story is the true story of being, and so speaks of that end toward which all human thought and every natural human act are originally oriented . . . it is indeed 'aesthetic' in the highest sense, a knowledge that is too intimately acquainted with what it knows ever to be reducible to mere explanation, but is also 'rational' in the highest sense, in that it can 'see' where and how other narratives fail the great theme of being, are to impoverished to speak the truth of reality's goodness, and simply lack the fullness and coherence that shows itself in the true.[58]

This is grounded in the recognition that beauty is a property of the Divine Being that exceeds every temporal instantiation (and recognition) of beauty. We gauge these historical appearances of beauty, including "beautiful" interpretations, by considering "the object held in one's regard, as well as the distance between the object and an infinite horizon [i.e., the Triune God]" and, therefore, "the object of attention, love, or awe is never finally, definitively *placed*, but is always serially consequent upon and open to an infinity of perspectives."[59] We read and interpret with reference to our contexts, the author's context, and the work—Jauss's triangle—but this is tempered by historical interpretations and beauty, which is possessed by the Infinite God, disclosed in the form of Christ, and in which every "true" interpretation participates.

With these observations in mind, the research below offers a selective reception history of 2 Thessalonians that illustrates the synchronic developments of interpretation at three epochal moments of the text's history. This should allow for greater appreciation of the aesthetic value of the respective

---

56. Candler describes this participatory reading as attempting to lead readers to a goal that is textual and ontological, but he also makes clear that the way of salvation is "furnished, not contained, by the text" (Candler, *Theology, Rhetoric, Manuduction*, 35, 45).

57. Hart, *Beauty of the Infinite*, 1.

58. Hart, *Beauty of the Infinite*, 31.

59. Hart, *Beauty of the Infinite*, 19.

interpretations. Diachrony shows the questions that have been asked in the historical dialogue with the text, but synchrony better illuminates why interpreters asked *particular* questions. It is hoped that a display of punctiliar enquiry aids the modern reader of scripture in formulating "good" questions in their reading. Further, it lends itself better to the present *possessing* of past questions that leads to greater self-understanding and, thereby, to speaking about what the letter "means."

In closing, restrictions enable us to offer an abbreviated *Rezeptionsästhetik* of 2 Thessalonians through a range of works, but this should hopefully demonstrate the importance of the program. The historically chronological progression of each chapter offers a diachronic image of the epistle's history, thus temporarily stabilizing a "canon" of 2 Thessalonians. Over against the authority of the modern reader and the "autonomy of the paragraph," this structure offers something of an enlarged glossed Bible and "recognizes the priority of the sequence of questions and responses."[60] Some familiarity with modern works on 2 Thessalonians expands the diachronic dimension of its history and provides a touchstone for gauging the aesthetic value of the pre-modern readings.[61] We turn now to fourth and fifth-century Byzantium and the Archbishop of Constantinople's reading of 2 Thessalonians.

---

60. Candler, *Theology, Rhetoric, Manuduction*, 36.

61. Arranging this project thusly does not bypass either the aesthetically perceptual reading or the reflectively interpretive reading. In the case of the first, it seems more appropriate to allow the reader to determine the aspects of 2 Thessalonians that they notice or prioritize. With the latter, interpretation may take place immediately in/after the first reading, but it also necessarily takes place and integrates material more fully after the "historical" reading, as Jauss himself shows when he reverses the order in his interpretation of Gen 3. See Jauss, *Question and Answer*, 95–100.

2

The Early Church
John Chrysostom

BACKGROUND

JOHN CHRYSOSTOM (349[1]–407) WAS born in the Syrian city of Antioch in the midst of great political, cultural, and ecclesiastical upheaval in the Byzantine Empire. Despite having lost his father at a young age, Chrysostom's social background saw that he was afforded the finest education available during his time. This instruction included finishing school with formal training in rhetoric, which he completed under the renowned pagan rhetor of Antioch, Libanius, alongside Theodore, the eventual bishop of Mopsuestia.[2] Though having the potential to pursue a successful career in public service, Chrysostom's Christian background[3] influenced his decision to receive baptism within a year of completing his studies (c. 367) and to take up service as an aide to Meletius, the pro-Nicene bishop of Antioch. In conjunction with this assignment, Chrysostom began frequenting a

---

1. Though historically debated, recent arguments favor John's birth date in the year 349. See especially Kelly, *Golden Mouth*, 296–98. See also Mayer and Allen, *John Chrysostom*, 3; Brändle, *Johannes Chrysostomus*, 13.

2. Kelly, *Golden Mouth*, 6–7; Brändle, *Johannes Chrysostomus*, 23; Pelikan, *Divine Rhetoric*, 16–18.

3. For this likelihood, see Kelly, *Golden Mouth*, 7.

local *askētērion* led by Diodore and Carterius, from whom he received a theological education and his initial exposure to asceticism.[4] By 371, he was elevated to the position of lector under Meletius, but he abandoned his duties to pursue an ascetic lifestyle in the Syrian wilderness shortly after his appointment. Meletius's exile for adherence to Nicene Trinitarianism around the same time likely accelerated Chrysostom's departure.[5]

During this retreat, Chrysostom spent four years taming his passions with a group of anchorite monks and an additional two years in isolation during which he applied himself to the memorisation of scripture. His extreme denial eventually led to severe renal and gastro-intestinal issues that would affect him for the rest of his life. This debilitation, coupled with Meletius's return, led Chrysostom back to Antioch, where he resumed his duties as a lector. Within two years he was ordained a deacon. And only five years thence he received ordination into the priesthood by Flavian, Meletius's successor.[6]

Chrysostom found himself as a priest and soul-carer for one of the largest and strategically most important cities in the Byzantine Empire.[7] It was a city marked by a drastic dichotomy between the wealthy echelon of society and the poorer constituents[8]—a characteristic that it shared with Chrysostom's later bishopric, Constantinople. For this reason, Chrysostom's sermons frequently feature the topics of wealth and the Christian necessity of almsgiving.[9] Chrysostom's elevation to bishop of Constantinople (397) after the sudden death of Nectarius meant that Chrysostom found the episcopal budget at his disposal, with which he was able to openly demonstrate the unity of his thought and praxis by quickly reconfiguring the expenditures and directing the primary funds away from ecclesiastical building projects toward hospitals, poorhouses, and similar charitable causes.[10] The combination of his confrontational character and his handling of episcopal power resulted in Chrysostom garnering powerful enemies in the ecclesial

---

4. For more on this educational period see Sterk, *Renouncing the World*, 142–44.

5. This was followed by an attempt to forcefully ordain Chrysostom into the priesthood, for which he considered himself unprepared. Kelly, *Golden Mouth*, 25–26.

6. Mayer and Allen, *John Chrysostom*, 5–7.

7. Brändle, *Johannes Chrysostomus*, 13.

8. Impoverished parents were even known to blind their children in order to evoke sympathy from passersby. Liebeschuetz, *Antioch*, 97–98.

9. Mayer and Allen, *John Chrysostom*, 46; Hartney, *John Chrysostom*, 133–70.

10. "God needs no golden goblets, but rather golden souls" (Brändle, *Johannes Chrysostomus*, 74–75).

(notably Theopholis, bishop of Alexandria) and political realms (e.g., princess Eudoxia). Collectively, these enemies rallied against the bishop and sentenced him to exile (*in absentia*) at the Synod of the Oak (403).[11] The uproar that resulted led to a rescission of the order by the emperor, which he reinstated in 404. This exile initially took Chrysostom to Cucusus in Armenia, but he was finally sent to Pityus on the eastern shore of the Black Sea, nearly 700 miles from Constantinople. Due to the speed of the journey and his already fragile health, Chrysostom died in transit (407).[12] Approximately 900 extant texts from Chrysostom have endured the passage of time, with the homilies[13] constituting the bulk of this collection.

Understanding the aesthetic value of Chrysostom's work requires the temporary stabilisation of a canon of texts from the early Church, with particular attention dedicated to authors from the Greek-speaking East and those from the Antiochene interpretive tradition. Situating it in this literary and historical context discloses the manner in which Chrysostom's reading of 2 Thessalonians confronted the horizon of expectations at his time, and how this reading can expand modern horizons of understanding.

Diachrony and The Synchronic Canon

As Jauss has shown, a key dimension to gauging the aesthetic value of a work comes from the literary horizons of the author's day. Works on 2 Thessalonians from John's time and region in particular come from Theodore of Mopsuestia, Theodoret of Cyrus, and Severian of Gabala. Other important literary works include those of earlier Fathers, such as Irenaeus, Origen, Evagrius Ponticus, and Tyconius, as well as those who reflect the influence of John—John Cassian, Augustine, Theophylact, the *Glossa Orinaria*, John of Damascus, and John Calvin. These will help to measure the aesthetic value and effect of John's work.

---

11. The events leading to Chrysostom's exile are complex and spread out over several years. For the list of factors and charges, see Kelly, *Golden Mouth*, 299–301; Liebeschuetz, *Barbarians and Bishops*, 198–222.

12. Mayer and Allen, *John Chrysostom*, 10–11; Chase, *Chrysostom*, 13–17.

13. Over 250 of these homilies are on the Pauline Epistles, excluding Galatians, for which Chrysostom offers a commentary.

THE EARLY CHURCH

2 Thessalonians Homilies: Provenance, Audience, Structure

For the purposes of this book, we look primarily at John's homilies on 2 Thessalonians with occasional insights from his other writings. Without certain details, the provenance of these and many of Chrysostom's works are difficult to determine.[14] Therefore, we situate the homilies generally in the context of a large, prosperous city in the Byzantine Empire. This also has some effect on the assumed audience of these homilies. If given in Constantinople, for example, much of the royal court, numerous monastics, and clergy would constitute part of the audience. Since the homilies do not appear to target these groups, however, we can assume a general audience that includes members from every social stratum.[15]

In terms of composition, we must also plead ignorance. Chrysostom may have composed the homilies in advance himself or preached extemporaneously with a stenographer recording. Even after the sermon, the homily would have been edited, with subsequent redactions occurring throughout the history of the text. Still, the texts maintain Chrysostom's rhetorical features, display consistency of character, and provide a lasting legacy.[16]

Chrysostom's homiletical structure varies according to the type of homily (e.g., exegetical, topical, polemical, or *encomium*), and the content hinges on the liturgical and civic calendars, topical events, catechesis, or more purely exegetical aims.[17] His homilies on the Pauline epistles are best classed as exegetical and follow a general, common structure. He often offers an introductory homily (*hypothesis*), which gives an overview and introduces key themes from the letter,[18] while the remaining homilies attend

---

14. For an in-depth evaluation of the dating of Chrysostom's homilies, see Mayer, *Homilies of St. John Chrysostom*.

15. For more on Chrysostom's audiences, see Mayer and Allen, *John Chrysostom*, 25–30.

16. Mayer and Allen, *John Chrysostom*, 30–31. The Migne text of the 2 Thessalonians homilies is considered relatively stable. For important variations, I have consulted the FCT.

17. Mayer and Allen, *John Chrysostom*, 21. These factors can even result in variations within a homiletical series. For example, Chrysostom's first homily on Genesis marks the beginning of Lent and focuses on fasting, employing Gen 2:16–17 late in the homily as a figurative reference to fasting (PG 53:23), while many of the remaining homilies proceed more exegetically through Genesis.

18. Young describes the introductory *hypothesis* and point-by-point examination of the text as characteristic of Antiochene interpretation. See Young, *Biblical Exegesis*, 171. Wilken adds that it is "shaped by historical setting, the author's intention, and literary

to consecutive sections of the epistle typically divided into two sections. The first and exegetical portion of the homily presents doctrine, while the "sermonic" section exhorts praxis.

Chrysostom's five homilies on 2 Thessalonians fit with the pattern described above.[19] The first homily, a *hypothesis*, offers a reconstruction of Paul's reasons for writing the letter: the Thessalonians feared the resurrection had passed and that the Judgment would soon follow because of the message of false teachers to this effect (correlating it with a similar situation in 2 Tim 2:1). The clear focus of 2 Thessalonians is to dispel this non-apostolic myth through a counter theology aimed at encouraging the Thessalonians in their current state of suffering as consistent with faith in Christ and by reasserting the events that must precede the resurrection, namely, the arrival of Antichrist. Before considering the homilies, however, we must also attend to key influences on John's reading.

Influential Impulses for Interpreting 2 Thessalonians

The instructive and rhetorical approach exhibited in his sermons reveal the salience with which John perceived the homily as "a powerful educative tool and medium of persuasion, as well as an effective means of forging a bond with those who actively listen to what he has to say."[20] He preached with "directness,"[21] avoiding the abstract, because of the conviction that the homily could profoundly affect social behaviour, promoting a form of ascetic-moralism in his congregations.[22]

---

character of the work" (Wilken, "*In novissimis diebus*," 148–49).

19. Of the Pauline epistles, Chrysostom's homilies on Romans, 1 Corinthians, Ephesians, Philippians, 1 Timothy, and Philemon share the same pattern of a *hypothesis* homily followed by exegetical homilies. The remaining Pauline epistles have no *hypothesis*, but maintain the bipartite, exegetical structure. See PG 60–62. The NT narrative homilies (Matt; John; Acts) also differ slightly from this pattern, though they tend to maintain the two-part structure exegesis and exhortation.

20. Mayer and Allen, *John Chrysostom*, 44.

21. Mayer and Allen, *John Chrysostom*, 27. Chrysostom owed his interpretive predilection to the instruction of Diodore, who criticised allegory sharply. See Kelly, *Golden Mouth*, 19.

22. Hartney, *John Chrysostom*, 33–34; Liebeschuetz, *Barbarians and Bishops*, 170, 181.

When looking specifically at Pauline texts, Chrysostom aims at perceiving the mind of the apostle[23] through the historical context of the given epistle and the rhetorical tools employed therein. Part of this task entails asking, "What is Paul doing as a pastor in this letter?" And Chrysostom works out the answer in terms of Christian formation. This materializes particularly in his repeated themes of wealth, pride, and humility.[24]

In his reading, Chrysostom strives to illuminate the meaning of the text by following Paul's "purpose" in the letter as a whole. At the same time, he sees the meaning of the text in the broader sense of God speaking presently in a way that has practical meaning for the congregation. So, though the Antiochene tradition emphasizes a literal reading of scripture, the canonical whole forms the interpretive context, which differs from the construal of "literal" interpretation in historical positivism.

Rather than explore his work according to homily and the order of 2 Thessalonians, we first examine aspects that shape Chrysostom's reading of the epistle, both in terms of literary and social context. These topics include: John's Antiochene exegetical heritage, his rhetorical education coupled with his esteem for Paul, and his asceticism, with the latter of these as the dominating influence. Combined with the literary expectations of his time, these elements constitute the horizon with which John approaches 2 Thessalonians.

Antiochene Exegetical Heritage

The Antiochene tradition of interpretation[25] both opens and delimits the direction of Chrysostom's interpretation. Generally speaking, the Antiochenes aimed to communicate the plain sense of the scripture, but this did not prevent them from perceiving spiritual insights toward which the text pointed with a method known as θεωρία. "For *theoria* to operate they considered it necessary (a) that the literal sense of the sacred narrative should not be abolished, (b) that there should be a real correspondence between

---

23. Chase, *Chrysostom*, 157.

24. Mayer and Allen, *John Chrysostom*, 21.

25. The Antiochene School can be divided into three periods according to its teachers. The first period began under under Lucian; the second, or "golden age," started with Diodore and extended through to the leadership of Theodore; the final "period of decay" came about through the association of Nestorius with Antioch. See Chase, *Chrysostom*, 2. Fairbairn and others have rightly argued against the clear-cut division of Antiochene and Alexandrian hermeneutics. See Fairbairn, "Patristic Exegesis and Theology," 1–19.

the historical fact and the further spiritual object discerned, and (c) that these two objects should be apprehended together, though of course in different ways."[26]

The larger aim of Antiochene exegesis, particularly under Diodore, was *paraenesis* and instruction. By attending to the "sense of the text, the aim of the speaker, the cause, and the occasion for the composition,"[27] the exegete is able to penetrate to the "hidden meaning"[28] of the passage. This offered something of a middle ground between the allegory of Alexandria and rigid literalism because it preserved "the text's underlying unity and logical coherence."[29] Chrysostom divides "Scriptural statements into (a) those which allow a 'theoretic' in addition to the literal sense, (b) those which are to be understood solely in the literal sense, and (c) those which admit only of a meaning other than the literal, i.e., allegorical statements."[30] Compared to allegory, θεωρία features quite prominently in his works. Though not with every verse, certainly with every homily Chrysostom reaches the stage of θεωρία if practical, present meaning can be included in the idea of θεωρία.[31] Neither the degree of interpretive flexibility nor the consistent arrival at θεωρία mark the commentaries of his contemporaries Diodore, Theodore of Mopsuestia, or Theodoret of Cyrus.

---

26. Kelly, *Early Christian Doctrines*, 76. See also Hughes, *Constructing Antichrist*, 51.

27. Wessel, *Cyril of Alexandria*, 250; cf. Chrysostom, *Against the Marcionists* 2 (*NPNF1* 9:201). Zaharopoulos describes *theoria* as presupposing *typology* rather than *allegory*, because allegory destroyed the historical significance of biblical narratives. Even Paul's own use of "allegory" to describe an illustration of Sarah and Hager (Gal 4:24) is employed "catachrestically," according to Chrysostom. See Zaharopoulos, *Theodore of Mopsuestia*, 112.

28. Chrysostom, *Against the Marcionists* 2 (*NPNF1* 9:201).

29. Wessel, *Cyril of Alexandria*, 250. Wallace-Hadrill contends that one of the main influences on Antiochene exegesis was the *mainstream* exegetical methodology of Jewish scholars, which held Philo at a distance (Wallace-Hadrill, *Christian Antioch*, 30).

30. Kelly, *Early Christian Doctrines*, 75.

31. Though variously and often inconsistently defined by the Fathers, Chrysostom's homiletical conclusions could be categorized as "a spiritual illumination in the mind of ... the later exegete" (Nassif, "Theōria," 1123). See Breck, *Scripture in Tradition*, 36–37. Young describes *historia*, as "pure" accounting, as the foundational lens through which scripture in Antiochene exegesis is read. *Theoria* has a mirroring coherence with the *historia* of the text, which differs from *allegoria* typified in the works of Origen and other Alexandrian exegetes. In the few cases of proper allegory in scripture, Chrysostom argues that the text always offers an explanation (see *Interpretatio in Isaiam prophetam* 5 [PG 56:60]). See Young, *Biblical Exegesis*, 176–82.

THE EARLY CHURCH

Other aspects characterizing Antiochene exegesis include questions of translation and etymology, attention to metaphorical language, and even comparisons of alternate readings. Much depends on the argument of the text and genre, which Antiochenes measure against other scriptures, and the background of the particular text in question, most often described in a *hypothesis*. As mentioned above, *paranaesis* held the primary place in exegesis with the overall aim of moral, ethical, and dogmatic exhortation.[32] Chrysostom overcomes the hermeneutical distance between his time and the text through this combined moral aim and θεωρία, drawing a parallel through the rhetorical intent of the text and the belonging of his own congregation to the biblical narrative.[33]

Reading Rhetorically with Paul

In addition to studying under Diodore, John also received thorough training in classical rhetoric. From the rhetorical schools came the primary emphasis on attention to the effect on the audience,[34] and included tools of the trade such as repetitions of a word or phrase at the beginning of a clause (*epaphanora*), anticipating audience answers, juxtaposition of phrases (*parison*), stating a point negatively then positively (*arsis*), pretended doubt (*diaporesis*), and the use of particular metaphors.[35]

Yet, the patristic era marks a definite shift in classical rhetoric to a more clearly delineated Christian rhetoric because of its reference and subject matter, with the Scriptural homily serving as an entirely "distinctive genre for Christian rhetoric."[36] So, John's division of each homily on 2 Thessalonians into two sections might be viewed as a rhetorical structure in general terms. Yet, this standard bipartite division actually betrays the esteem in which Chrysostom holds Paul, because it is modelled after a pattern he sees the apostle's letters.[37] Nevertheless, his imitation can be traced in part to his rhetorical education, for a skilled rhetor follows the example of those who precede him, and it inculcates attention to structural

32. This was viewed as the purpose of reading and rhetoric in Chrysostom's day. Young, *Biblical Exegesis*, 81, 248.
33. Young, *Biblical Exegesis*, 171–73, 248–54.
34. Young, *Biblical Exegesis*, 81, 253.
35. Mayer and Allen, *John Chrysostom*, 20–21; Mitchell, *Heavenly Trumpet*, 25.
36. Pelikan, *Divine Rhetoric*, 31; cf. 3–33.
37. Chase, *Chrysostom*, 155; Young, *Biblical Exegesis*, 254–55.

and methodological detail. His rhetorical education does not result in a strict adherence to Greco-Roman rhetoric, but rather that it heightens his awareness of Paul's rhetoric and better enables him to make use of it for his own homiletical purposes.

As Mitchell's work on Chrysostom has shown, the apostle Paul exerts a commanding influence on John.[38] An obvious example of his regard for Paul appears in his seven *encomia* on the apostle (PG 50:477–514), which Mitchell classifies as a form of epideictic rhetoric that extols a person in a threefold division of praise for the individual's "body, soul, and external circumstances."[39] This form of rhetoric, as an exegetical endeavour, does not simply describe the person in question, but aims at persuading the audience to adopt what has been praised. Thus, Paul's program of "imitation" (1 Cor 4:16; 11:1; Phil 3:17; 1 Thess 1:6–7) aligns well with this strand of classical rhetoric, and Chrysostom advances it to the fore.[40] Beyond the *encomia*, and throughout the entire corpus of his work, however, Paul continually materializes as "example, authority, conversation partner, and icon."[41] Additionally, Chrysostom clearly perceives the overlap between the his own life and the apostle's, as one forcefully placed into Christian ministry, constantly addressing contentious pastoral issues, and ending his life in exile.[42]

Ascetic Influences

All of the above influences on the 2 Thessalonians homilies can be subsumed under John's ascetic background and its contours. John's homiletical work must be seen in light of his foundational years in the *askētērion* of Diodore and Carterios and his monastic retreat to the region of Silpios.[43] This way of life is shaped by emphases on certain biblical impulses, especially the rhetoric of "the proud and the humble" that features especially in

---

38. The affection for Paul might be traced in part to his Antiochene provenance, where Paul was a favoured saint alongside Peter. John Chrysostom, *Homilia in Acta* 25 (PG 60:192); Mitchell, *Heavenly Trumpet*, 67.

39. Mitchell, *Heavenly Trumpet*, 98. See also 404–7 for a distinction between encomium and vita.

40. Mitchell, *Heavenly Trumpet*, 49–55.

41. Mitchell, *Heavenly Trumpet*, 5.

42. Mitchell, *Heavenly Trumpet*, 68.

43. Kelly, *Golden Mouth*, 18–29.

the Psalms, Sirach, and its eschatological rendering in the NT. Antiochene asceticism is, therefore, marked by an eschatologically-oriented present in thought and action, constant redirection of attention to God, the promotion of humility, and the renunciation of making money.[44]

In terms of *unmitigated influence* this pedagogical background hones his vision to perceive, particularly, the issues of *pride* and *concern for the poor* with unclouded clarity. John reads 2 Thessalonians through the ascetic-theological lens of virtue and vice. This theological contrast structures our discussion below as John moves from describing Paul as the virtuous example to imitate, to the Thessalonian Christians as those who are cultivating virtuous habits, to the "vicious" and their touchstone: the Antichrist.

THE VIRTUOUS APOSTLE

In his *hypothesis* homily on 2 Thessalonians John lays out two catalysts for the epistle's composition. Primarily, the devil "took a different path" from teaching a false doctrine by means of "certain corrupt people . . . who said that the resurrection had already happened" in the first epistle to circulating the idea that "the Judgment and Christ's [P]arousia were imminent."[45] Therefore, Paul had to correct a dogmatic issue concerning the *eschaton*. Secondly, through this correction and the letter at large, Paul hoped to encourage the faithful so that they "might [not] faint on account of [their] sufferings."[46] In this process, John focuses on the dominating presence of the Antichrist in the letter how it reveals this character as "anointed unto pride."[47] Being the chief characteristic of the Antichrist, John warns his congregation to avoid and dispel pride at all costs so as not to "fall into his condemnation."[48] He perceives this despite the fact that the term "pride" never appears in 2 Thessalonians. By introducing "pride," John begins an ascetic-theological reading of the epistle that will contrast Paul and Christian virtue with the vice/passion of the Antichrist.

---

44. Kelly, *Golden Mouth*, 18; Mayer and Allen, *John Chrysostom*, 28.
45. "ὁ διάβολος . . . ἑτέραν ἦλθεν ὁδόν, καὶ καταθεὶς ἀνθρώπους τινὰς λυμεῶνας . . . Τότε μὲν οὖν ἔλεγον ἐκεῖνοι τὴν ἀνάστασιν ἤδη γεγονέναι" (John Chrysostom, *In epist. ii ad Thess* 1 [PG 62:468]).
46. John Chrysostom, *In epist. ii ad Thess* 1 (PG 62:468).
47. John Chrysostom, *Homilies on 2 Thesss* 1 (*NPNF1* 13:378).
48. John Chrysostom, *In epist. ii ad Thess* 1 (PG 62:470).

Turning to the opening of the letter, John directs attention to the thanksgiving "We are bound to give thanks to God for you, brothers, as is right" (1:3a), and calls his congregation to "witness [the] excess of humility"[49] in the apostle. For the thanksgiving is given to God for the good actions of the Thessalonians, which, John contends, should be the hope of every Christian—that in seeing the good of the believer, people are directed to God, not the one performing the good. In this way, Paul becomes the example to imitate.

Theodore likewise comments on 2 Thess 1:3a, though he takes it as an extension of the grace from the previous verse. He does not perceive this as a humble expression on the part of Paul, but rather it indicates how great the behaviour of the Thessalonians must be for Paul to give thanks to God for them. Therefore, this thanksgiving directs one's attention to the greatness of what follows this verse: the reason(s) for the thanksgiving.[50] Theodoret follows his predecessor at Antioch by focusing on the impulse for the thanksgiving, namely their "perfect virtue"[51] demonstrated in their faith and love, rather than the direction of the thanksgiving to God and the character of Paul for such an emphasis. The Thessalonians are the exemplars for Theodoret. Different from both, John of Damascus concentrates solely on the traits of faith and love that Paul commends.[52]

John provokes the contemporary horizon of expectations with an interpretation that shifts the reader's focus to a theological principle based on the structure of the text. Reading against the grain of history helps recover the distinctiveness of John's voice, which offers another perspective of the text from modern interpreters without doing it violence.[53]

---

49. "Ὅρα ταπεινοφροσύνης ὑπερβολήν" (John Chrysostom, *In epist. ii ad Thess* 2 [PG 62:473]). In painting such a "portrait" of Paul, John is summoning his hearers to mimesis. See Mitchell, *Heavenly Trumpet*, 51.

50. Theodore of Mopsuestia, "In epist. ii Thess," 42–43.

51. Theodoret of Cyrus, "2 Thessalonians," 126.

52. John of Damascus, *In epist. ii ad Thess* (PG 95:920)

53. Scholars as early as Paul Schubert regard John's reading of the thanksgiving as making too much out of a stylistic feature of Greco-Roman epistles. See Schubert, *Form and Function*. Thiselton, however, helpfully remarks on the importance of observing the difference between the "*expected* convention of the thanksgiving form and Paul's *distinctive* use of it" (Thiselton, *First Epistle*, 87). O'Brien supplements this by noting the functional importance of the thanksgiving for Paul's message and that it would not be unnatural to assume that Paul was *actually* thankful to God for the reasons he mentions in the letter. See O'Brien, "Thanksgiving and the Gospel," 145–46. For a more in-depth discussion, see O'Brien, *Introductory Thanksgivings*.

Later in the same homily, John cites the fearful description of the Lord arriving "in flaming fire, inflicting vengeance on those who do not know God" (1:8) as a means of encouragement to the Thessalonians to know that by their faithfulness they will avoid the "condemnation and vengeance"[54] of hell experienced by their afflicters. Further, it encourages them to endure affliction. John comments, however, that ὁ σφόδρα ἐνάρετος (the exceedingly virtuous one) is not compelled to virtue through fear of hell or "the prospect of the kingdom, but on account of Christ himself; just as Paul was."[55] Within the early Church's virtue-matrix of faith, hope, and love, with the last of these reflecting the height of virtue, Christians on varying stages of maturity are compelled to obedience through one of the above traits.[56] This verse describes both the doctrine of the final Judgment and functions as an aid for those on a lower stratum of virtue (faith) until they graduate to subsistence in "perfect love"[57] for the sake of Christ alone. Paul is ὁ σφόδρα ἐνάρετος.

This point on the character of Paul resurfaces when John proposes that Christians hold this terrifying doctrine of hell and judgment constantly before their eyes. Again, he suggests this as a transitional stage in the Christian life that should eventually lead to despising all things, including hell, in the same manner as Paul. John chastizes his congregation and himself for not even being willing to bear a discourse on hell, which is for their advantage, while Paul despises it altogether for "the sake of the love of Christ."[58] A shift away from reading the NT theologically accounts for

---

54. John Chrysostom, *In epist. ii ad Thess* 2 (PG 62:476).

55. John Chrysostom, *In epist. ii ad Thess* 2 (PG 62:476).

56. This matrix is largely built upon 1 Cor 13:13, but the early Church also substantiated this perspective with 1 Thess 1:3; 5:8 (cf. 2 Thess 1:3, which omits "hope"); Heb 10:22-24; 1 Pet 1:20-23. See Augustine, *Enchiridion on Faith, Hope, and Love*; *On Christian Doctrine* 1:39:43 (NPNF1 2:534); *Treatise on Grace and Free Will* 34-38 (NPNF1 5:458-60); John Cassian, *Conferences* 11:6-13 (NPNF2 11:416-422); Cyprian of Carthage, *Treatises* 1:14 (ANF 5:425-26); Clement of Alexandria, *Stromata* 4:7 (PG 8:1264-65). See especially Cassian and Clement, who appear to substitute "faith" with "fear" in a manner quite consistent with John.

57. Different from theologians like Basil, John places "perfection of love within the reach of every Christian," thus universalizing what was often reserved for the ascetics (Osborn, "Love," 695). John proffers similar comments in John Chrysostom, *Homilies on 1 Corinthians* 34:5 (NPNF1 12:203-204). He also elevates love above faith in John Chrysostom, *Homilies on Hebrews* 19 (NPNF1 14:454-57).

58. John Chrysostom, *In epist. ii ad Thess* 2, 478.

the vanishing of John's voice on this point and an emphasis on authorial intention renders it difficult to revive.

The Virtuous Christian

In this ascetic-theological reading, John attends to both Paul as the virtuous model and the "faithful," first readers of the letter, who are developing in virtue, but are not at the level of ὁ σφόδρα ἐνάρετος. John makes use of Paul's rhetorical strategy of teaching the Thessalonians to likewise train his congregation. In this process, John attends to the rhetorical training of heart and mind through the apostle's thanksgiving for virtues and the sure promise of divine judgment, but he extends this with considerations of martyrdom and treatment of the poor, which likewise fit into Paul (and John's) rhetorical strategy.

Regarding the opening thanksgiving again, John notes the rhetorical function of Paul's language: "we ought always to give thanks to God for you brothers, as is right" (1:3). By such an expression, "he lifts their spirits, because their suffering is not worthy of weeping and lamenting, but rather of thanksgiving to God."[59] That is to say, by thanking God for the Thessalonians for their enduring faith in suffering, Paul encourages the congregation. Furthermore, this thanksgiving directs their minds away from themselves and toward God, forcing them to consider that someone's good actions ought to cause others to admire God before the individual. Paul and John are offering habit-forming ways of speaking and thinking that lead to virtues like thankfulness and an overall orientation toward the Good.

John concludes his exhortation for virtue with the broader emphasis on the authority of scripture. In relation to the content of 2 Thessalonians, according to John, this means that the realisation of the Divine source should cast out all pride from the Christian,[60] especially when the reader/hearer comprehends that pride is a characteristic of Antichrist.[61] Furthermore, as Christ corrects the slothful in Thessalonica through Paul (2 Thess 3:6–13), so he continues to do so with the current reader.[62] This perspective of scripture's origin must necessarily have a reality-shaping effect on the Christian community such that the lives of Christians cohere with the

59. John Chrysostom, *In epist. ii ad Thess* 2 (PG 62:473).
60. John Chrysostom, *In epist. ii ad Thess* 3 (PG 62:484).
61. John Chrysostom, *In epist. ii ad Thess* 1 (PG 62:470).
62. John Chrysostom, *In epist. ii ad Thess* 3 (PG 62:484–85).

divine discourse—particularly as it relates to Christ's Lordship and reverent fear of God as God.[63] For this reason, Paul's question to the Thessalonians about their memory of instruction already given (2:5) leads John into a discussion regarding the importance of repeated biblical instruction as a means to dehydrate and destroy the thorny roots of sin through the application of these "fiery" texts on the coming judgment.[64] John does not draw an analogy between the text and his present, but concentrates his congregation's attention on the extra-contextual promise of judgment.

Theodore omits the former point regarding encouragement, but expands the latter, noting that thanksgiving is obligatory and further reveals the Thessalonians' need for the grace of God.[65] Theodoret, however, appears not to notice the direction or the obligation of the thanksgiving and, though he describes it as a εὐφημία, he does not question the response that Paul strives to evoke in the Thessalonian church.[66] Though all three certainly had rhetorical training, John's homiletical focus causes him to consider the evocative nature of the epistle.

From the Western Church around this time we might also add Augustine's reading,[67] in which he notes that Paul attaches the obligation as an addendum to the grace "lest they should make a boast of the great good which they were enjoying from God, as if they had it of their own mere selves."[68] Augustine's doctrinal concerns generally guide his reading, yet his rhetorical training pierces through the surface as he notes a different dimension of this statement. On the one hand, according to John, this verse encourages believers to remain in the faith during persecution, on the other

63. John Chrysostom, *In epist. ii ad Thess* 3 (PG 62:484).

64. John Chrysostom, *In epist. ii ad Thess* 3 (PG 62:483).

65. Theodore of Mopsuestia, "In epist. ii Thess," 43. See also Thiselton, *1 and 2 Thessalonians*, 182.

66. Theodoret of Cyrus, *Epist. ii ad Thess* (PG 82:660).

67. Cooper has confidently shown that Anianus of Celeda translated many of Chrysostom's works into Latin within ten to fourteen years of Chrysostom's death (Cooper, "An(n)ianus of Celeda," 249–55). Altaner traces a relationship between Augustine and John several decades prior to Cooper (Altaner, "Augustinus und Johannes Chrysostomus," 76–84). Augustine interacted with the work of the bishop in *Against Julian* within two decades of Chrysostom's death. On one occasion, Augustine rebuffs Julian of Eclanum's use of John by enlisting John to support his position that infants do not have sins of their own, but that does not preclude the effect of original sin (Augustine, *Against Julian* [FC 35:25–35, esp. 27]).

68. Augustine, *On Grace and Free Will* 38 (NPNF1 5:460). *Against Julian* predates this treatise by several years.

hand, according to Augustine, the verse reminds them that God enables their faith and perseverance by his grace. What John only hints at by noting that one's good actions ought to cause others to admire God, Augustine makes more explicit by revealing God as the source of those good things. If John influences Augustine's reading of 2 Thessalonians in any way, one can assume that it is unilateral.[69]

John's dual reading considers both the ultimate source and aim of the thanksgiving and the rhetorical effect that the reading of this thanksgiving will have on the Thessalonian church. Reintegrating this into the discussion of 2 Thessalonians would broaden the horizon of understanding to push beyond Greco-Roman epistolary practices and semantics to a more theologically-constrained, virtuous reading of the epistle.

John's eventual attention to the description of the judgment in "flaming fire" and "vengeance" (1:8) leads into encouragement and paraenesis for his own community. Paul's encouragement to the Thessalonians becomes the encouragement for future congregations: "Therefore, when we are in affliction, let us consider these things."[70] Beyond this, however, the epistle provides a description of hell that Christians ought always consider, "for no one holding hell before their eyes will fall into hell."[71] The bishop indicates further how Paul stokes the fire of virtue by reaching out to the Thessalonians, distraught in their affliction, and praising them for their endurance and comforting them with the hope of the future. Rhetorically (and collectively), these elements encourage the Thessalonians to remain resolute in their faith. Chrysostom adds that Paul includes the detailed description of Antichrist in this letter to buttress his encouragement, "For the weak soul is quite fully assured, not simply when it hears [about something], but when it learns something in detail."[72] The bishop looks at the text in terms of both *meaning* and the *function*, especially for his own congregation.

Theodoret appears to follow Chrysostom directly in reading this as comfort by means of future expectation, even using the same term, τῶν

---

69. Best breaks from this interpretation by commenting that the obligation arises out of Paul's personal relationship with the Thessalonians rather than out of "the nature of things" (Best, *Thessalonians*, 249). See also Fee, *Thessalonians*, 248. Both of these scholars follow Rigaux who draws a distinction between the use of ὀφείλω, which is personal, and δεῖ which "est dans la nature des choses" (Rigaux, *Thessaloniciens*, 613).

70. John Chrysostom, *In epist. ii ad Thess* 2 (PG 62:476).

71. John Chrysostom, *In epist. ii ad Thess* 2 (PG 62:477).

72. John Chrysostom, *In epist. ii ad Thess* 1 (PG 62:469). This unfolding of Paul's rhetoric should also have an effect on Chrysostom's readers.

μελλόντων,[73] as Chrysostom. Severian as well notes the comfort extended by (future) "justice and great reward of Christ."[74] It is possible that this was simply a common idea applied to 2 Thessalonians at the time, however, Theodore omits such a note in his *argumentum*.

Looking more generally at 2 Thess 1 and Paul's discussion of the Day of the Lord, John is concerned that doctrines of the resurrection, the Judgment, the coming of Antichrist, and the biblical description of hell shape the virtuous life.[75] This turn from abstract dogma occurs in his description of false doctrines, sown by Satan, growing up in a person, so that they manipulate their worldview and lead to the neglect of biblical exhortation (e.g., the renunciation of pride).[76]

John forcefully urges that the doctrine relating to the *eschaton* must affect the Christian living in the present. In truth, he desires that all Christians be compelled by the love of Christ (like Paul) into living in a manner consistent with the reality revealed in scripture.[77] Yet until that compulsion develops, he points to the terrifying doctrine regarding the judgment of the wicked and punishment in hell as a means of shaping the way that one views his/herself. The terrifying description of God's eschatological wrath means, for Chrysostom, that one ought to live in a manner properly oriented to this end. It is more than awareness; it is living acknowledgement.[78] The emphasis on hell alone provokes the modern (Western) horizon, which tends to neglect or diminish this doctrine because of its offensiveness.

Elsewhere, John makes note of the vengeance coming to the wicked (1:8), and insists that it encourages those who are afflicted because it demonstrates the justice of God, but that it should not be a cause for the Christian to rejoice. Instead, he attempts to ground his congregation in the awareness that their salvation is one of grace, not merit. Furthermore, they ought to develop such thinking by concentrating on the blessing of the promised kingdom and the fearful reality of hell. In fact, Christians should concentrate more on the judgment and hell than the kingdom as a

---

73. Even the form of the verb is the same in the two works; John Chrysostom, *In epist. ii ad Thess* 1 (PG 62:469); Theodoret of Cyrus, *In epist. ii ad Thess* (PG 82:657). The idea of *encouragement* by means "of the future hope" is clearer in Theodoret than in Chrysostom.

74. Severian von Gabala, "Fragmenta," 332.

75. John Chrysostom, *2 Thessalonians* 1 (NPNF1 13:377–79).

76. John Chrysostom, *2 Thessalonians* 1 (NPNF1 13:379).

77. John Chrysostom, *2 Thessalonians* 2 (NPNF1 13:382, 383).

78. John Chrysostom, *2 Thessalonians* 1 (NPNF1 13:379–80).

means of shaping their lives, "for fear has more power than the promise,"[79] especially for the "infants" of the faith. The provocation mentioned above is sharpened by this emphasis.

The holding of appropriate fear appears in the *Martyrdom of Polycarp* when, in his dialogue with the proconsul, Polycarp dismisses the threat of death by means of the flaming pyre: "You threaten with a fire that burns for an hour and after a short while is extinguished; for you do not know about the fire of the coming judgment and eternal torment, reserved for the ungodly."[80]

Irenaeus quotes the entirety of 2 Thess 1:7–10 as evidence against Gnostic groups who speak incessantly about the mercy of the Lord in the NT and neglect the passages referring to his Judgment, so as to defend their belief that the demiurge is the god of the OT and entirely distinct from the Son and Father of the NT.[81] For Irenaeus, teaching on the wrath of God in the Judgment is an essential part of Christian instruction. Similarly, Ephrem the Syrian (d. 373) points out that though the Lord tends to offer help in the form of persuasion, he also reproves with fearful means, like the "flaming fire" of the coming judgment (1:8).[82]

Of his Antiochene contemporaries, however, Theodoret sees the fearsome nature of the coming Judgment only as a means of encouraging the afflicted. He does not take the next step in turning it into a warning for Christians from falling away, or for forgetting their existence in a state of grace, or for the cultivation of virtue.[83] The fragmentary nature of Severian's commentary confirms that he agrees with Theodoret, but it is uncertain as to whether he sees the dimension of fear that this description of the Judgment should instil in Christians. His view of the event as an encouragement to the afflicted Thessalonians because it is punishment for their having been wronged,[84] however, make it likely that he did not read

---

79. "μᾶλλον γὰρ ὁ φόβος ἰσχύει τῆς ἐπαγγελίας" (John Chrysostom, *In epist. ii ad Thess* 2 [PG 62:477]).

80. *Martyrdom of Polycarp* 11.2. See also the introduction to "Martyrdom of Polycarp" in *Apostolic Fathers*, 383.

81. Irenaeus, *Against Heresies* 4.27.4 (ANF 1:501); Thiselton, *1 and 2 Thessalonians*, 193.

82. Raised in the same region as Chrysostom, it is important to note both his shared view of scripture for reproof and his understanding of "the Lord" as the source of all scripture. Ephraim Syrus, *Three Homilies* 1.22 (NPNF2 13:314).

83. Theodoret of Cyrus, "2 Thessalonians," 126–27.

84. Severian von Gabala, "Fragmenta," 332.

this like John, who sees the Judgment as grounded in agnosticism and lack of response to the gospel (1:8), or, put differently, God's concern for his own glory.[85]

Though writing without a particular reference to 2 Thessalonians, Basil shares this perspective of living in the fear of the Lord. In a letter to a widow (c. 374), Basil reminds the woman that "to whomsoever there is present the vivid expectation of the threatened punishments, the fear which dwells in such will give them no opportunity of *falling into* ill-considered actions."[86] The striking resemblance of this language reveals that Chrysostom has taken up a common discourse in the early Church, which is particularly appropriate to the tone of 2 Thessalonians and his view of "being worthy of calling" as a summons to martyrdom. Perhaps the only element that surpasses his horizon is his emphasis on divine grace.

Generations later, Calvin remains faithful to Chrysostom's concern that the fearful doctrine of the Judgment and hell not be diminished. He avers, "Christ will avenge with the strictest severities the wrongs which the wicked inflict upon us."[87] He adds to this the note that God punishes the rebellious "for the sake of his own glory,"[88] echoing Chrysostom, though this reading fits naturally with Calvin's theology. He concentrates further on the terrible nature of hell in terms of its eternal duration, which signals that "the violent nature of that death will never cease."[89]

Returning to John, another example of cultivating virtue from 2 Thess 1 reflects his rhetorical training and his Antiochene background as he reads "that God might make/deem you worthy (ἀξιώσῃ) of the calling" (1:11). He contends that this indicates the "call" is neither God's ultimate permission to enter the kingdom of heaven at the *eschaton*, nor the past calling into a life of discipleship that leads ultimately to salvation. Instead, he connects being "made worthy" with "every work of faith" (1:11), which he describes as "the patient endurance of persecutions."[90] This coincides with his reading of being "counted worthy (καταξιωθῆναι) of the kingdom of God, for which you also suffer" (1:5).

---

85. "δι' ἑαυτὸν ἀνάγκη τιμωρήσασθαι αὐτός" (John Chrysostom, *In epist. ii ad Thess* 2 [FCT 5:455]).

86. Basil of Caesarea, *Letters*, 174 (emphasis added).

87. Calvin, *Epistles of Paul*, 391.

88. Calvin, *Epistles of Paul*, 391.

89. Calvin, *Epistles of Paul*, 392.

90. John Chrysostom, *In epist. ii ad Thess* 3 (PG 62:480).

What sets Chrysostom's exegesis apart, however, is his connecting ἀξιώσῃ and κλῆσις, and his contention that the Thessalonians "were not called."[91] The latter point has the rhetorical effect of keeping the readers from becoming prideful. The former point appears to work under several assumptions. In the first case, being "made/deemed worthy" could simply refer to persecution that one suffers in the name of Christ. Being "made/deemed worthy *of calling*," however, is that calling to the "bride-chamber" (ὁ νυμφίος); an indication that Chrysostom understands this passage as a reference to martyrdom. This perspective is strengthened by Chrysostom's quotation of Heb 12:4. Only in this way, can the Thessalonians be at the full "persuasion" (πεῖσμα) of God. Chrysostom's reading reflects the elevated view of martyrdom in the early Church, which understood martyrs as entering immediately into the presence, or "bride-chamber," of God.[92] Therefore, the bishop confidently contends that the Thessalonians have not yet been called.[93] This absence of "calling" functions as a sober reminder to prevent them from becoming "slothful"—a rhetorical strategy to encourage their remaining in the faith and to submit to the πεῖσμα of God.[94]

This reading differs starkly from those of his contemporaries. Theodore, for example, notes that the calling has occurred by means of the preaching of the gospel and, though it is the call to a salvific end in the *eschaton*, the Thessalonians responded to that call prior to the authorship of this epistle. It is possible to fall away from a type of calling, as Chrysostom

---

91. John Chrysostom, *In epist. ii ad Thess* 3 (PG 62:480).

92. Both the language of being "made worthy" and immediate translation into the "presence of God" is found in the *Martyrdom of Polycarp* 13.2, thus indicating the early development of this perspective. Similar connections of martyrdom and the "bridal-chamber" appear in Methodius, *Banquet of the Ten Virgins* 7.3 (ANF 6:332); Leo the Great, *Letters* 98.3 (NPNF2 12:73); Chrysostom, *Homilies on S. Ignatius and S. Babylas* (*NPNF1* 9:135–43). We should here add that Chrysostom connects 2 Thessalonians with the Synoptic Apocalypse and the language of Matt 25:1–13.

93. The FCT and the CGPNT (6.384) read "οὐ γὰρ ἐκλήθησαν." The PG text reads "δεικνὺς ὅτι πολλοὶ καὶ ἀπεβλήθησαν." It is likely that Migne's source misses the implicit understanding of martyrdom and attempted to resolve the difficulty of this reading through redaction. The difference in the above phrase and the absence of "But he speaks of that other calling" (Ἀλλ' ἐκείνην τὴν κλῆσίν φησι) from the PG text means that the Migne text attempts to reconstrue "calling" as an eschatological goal, but this renders the text awkward. See John Chrysostom, *2 Thessalonians* 3 (NPNF1 13:385); *In epist. ii ad Thess* 3 (FCT 5:463); *In epist. ii ad Thess* 3 (PG 62:480).

94. John Chrysostom, *In epist. ii ad Thess* 3 (PG 62:480).

warns, but Thedore perceives the calling as having already taken place and does not connect it with martyrdom.⁹⁵

Theodoret essentially reiterates Theodore, though he concentrates on the nature of this prayer for the Thessalonians to produce endurance in persecution so that they will remain in the calling.⁹⁶ John of Damascus even follows John's rhetorical understanding that this verse keeps the Thessalonians, as well as modern readers, from thinking too highly of themselves in their perseverance and good works. This does not, however, deny that they have been called, but describes God as an "assistant" (συλλήπτωρ) in accomplishing "every desire of goodness and work of faith" (1:11) *after* the have been called.⁹⁷

In the tenth century, Thietland of Einsiedeln initially pursues a similar reading to that of Chrysostom. He contends that, by his grace, God considered the Thessalonians "worthy" of his Kingdom (1:5), not because they suffered persecution.⁹⁸ Yet Thietland does not connect this concept of worthiness with God making the Thessalonians "worthy of calling" (1:11). He still establishes this worthiness in the grace of God, but thinks of "calling" in terms of a purpose.⁹⁹

The anomalous nature of Chrysostom's reading likely accounts for its near immediate disappearance from exegetical consideration as well as its absence from the *Glossa Ordinaria*.¹⁰⁰ At the same time, tradition does

---

95. Theodore of Mopsuestia, "In epist. ii Thess," 47–48.

96. "ὥστε ὑμᾶς ἀξιωθέντας τῆς κλήσεως" (Theodoret of Cyrus, *Epist. ii ad Thess* [PG 82:661]). Hill translates this as "you have been granted the call"—bringing out the aorist-passive sense of Theodore's reading. See Theodoret of Cyrus, "2 Thessalonians," 127.

97. John of Damascus, *In epist. ii ad Thess* (PG 95:921)

98. Thietland of Einselden, "In epist. ii ad Thess," 43–44.

99. Thietland of Einselden, "In epist. ii ad Thess," 48–49. Wanamaker agrees that the prayer is for the salvation of Paul's readers on the day of judgment, but he remains somewhat vague regarding the time of the call; describing it simply as "God's call to the Thessalonians to share in eschatological salvation" (Wanamaker, *Thessalonians*, 233). Best weighs out only two possible readings of ἀξιώσῃ in terms of time, pointing out that reading it as "deem worthy" locates the action in the eschaton, whereas "make worthy" has the connotation of a process involving the participation of God, as John of Damascus saw it. In the end, he reads it as "make worthy," but qualifies that only God can help achieve this and that it leads to a salvific end (Best, *Thessalonians*, 268–69). Fee echoes this two-fold option, but notes that the rest of the sentence leads one to read it as "make worthy" (Fee, *Thessalonians*, 264). Rigaux likewise prefers reading it as "make worthy" because it fits with the intimate nature of the prayer (1:11–12) in which this phrase is situated (Rigaux, *Thessaloniciens*, 639).

100. The *Glossa* includes Chrysostom's comments on 1:10. See de Lyra, *Glossa*

not always carry forward every question posed to the text because many are "erased by a definitive answer, others forgotten, renewed once more, or posed only at a comparatively late date."[101] It appears that Chrysostom's question of the relationship of worthiness, calling, and martyrdom is a potential victim of either of the former two categories and a shift in Christian society from occasional martyrdom under pagan rulers to post-Constantine security. The relatively stable interpretive options on this passage, however, do not rescind Chrysostom's aesthetically valuable reading.

One might expect John's accounting of pride to end with the material on the man of lawlessness, but he extends the discussion in a unique manner to the end of the epistle: concern for the poor. In his first homily on 2 Thessalonians, the bishop sees that pride quickly leads to an unhealthy thirst for wealth and a reciprocal contempt for the poor,[102] though without specifying the "type" of poor. The discussion of the poor resurfaces with greater attention in his final homily on the epistle. On its own, the topic does not appear to have any relationship to the content of the letter. It grows out of reading scripture that is both conscious of social context and an ascetic-moralism that has a developed and holistic understanding of practices described in scripture.

In the first homily, the concern remains general: Chrysostom wants his congregation to expel pride, so that they might be appropriately concerned for the poor in general. He substantiates this in his sermon on almsgiving, in which he pleads with his congregants to give as scripture compels them after he witnesses penury in the winter marketplace.[103]

In his fifth homily, John perceives Paul as working night and day (2 Thess 3:8) *in order "to assist"*[104] *others*. In this way, Paul provides an example in how Christians should work and to what end (i.e., both to keep from being idle and to provide for those in need)[105] thereby uniting the issues of idleness and poverty. Chrysostom sharpens his chastisement of the

---

Ordinaria, 6:668.

101. Jauss, *Question and Answer*, 70.

102. John Chrysostom, *2 Thessalonians* 2 (*NPNF1* 13:382).

103. John Chrysostom, *On Repentance and Almsgiving* (FC 96:131–49).

104. "ἐπικουρεῖν" (John Chrysostom, *In epist. ii ad Thess* 5 [PG 62:494]).

105. As he has laid the groundwork in his first homily for understanding every sin as proceeding from and sustained by pride, the discussion on the topic of sin and almsgiving should not be understood as separate.

congregants for insulting the beggar "who for your sake is poor,"[106] rather than giving and admonishing privately, as Paul instructed (3:15).[107] He is clearly speaking of poor Christians at this point, and especially monks, who have renounced both wealth and work. These monastic "idle" are not likely so because they believe the Day of the Lord is imminent, as in Paul's day, but because the degree of their poverty necessitates their begging, even in the case of those who exert themselves constantly in spiritual work rather than physical work by which they can earn a living.

Situating this in the literary context of John's day, we see how far he extends ascetic-morality and instruction to his congregants. In his *Longer Rules* for monastic communities, Basil not only makes an explicit connection between pride and idleness,[108] he also asserts that the "aim and intention with which the workers [monks] must work" is to provide for "those in want, not his own need."[109] Like John, he grounds this in Paul's exhortation and reminder to the Thessalonians to follow the example that he gave them, quoting 2 Thess 3:8, 11–12. Further, the life of voluntary mendicant poverty was intended as a means of purging pride and cultivating humility, which also connects Basil's thought world to John's. Both authors mine the text for doctrine. For one it relates particularly to governance of monastic communities, but to the other the exhortation applies equally to all Christians.[110]

Likewise regulating monastic communities, John Cassian pursues a similar tack as Basil and Chrysostom, though he expands the discussion and follows his master, Evagrius Ponticus,[111] by situating it in the discourse of the eight *logismoi*. Under the spirit of *acedia* (weariness) Cassian

---

106. The assumption here being that God allows the person to be poor for the sake of the giver's own "healing." John Chrysostom, *In epist. ii ad Thess* 5 (PG 62:496)

107. Generally speaking, reactions to the structurally poor bordered on hostile. Reactions to the voluntary poor varied from kindness to mistreatment like those above. Chrysostom's challenge to his congregation to give generously to the poor (particularly the structurally poor) was a battle against the cultural ethos of viewing the poor with suspicion. See Mayer, "Poverty and Generosity," 140–58. Brändle argues that Chrysostom makes almsgiving a soteriological issue, looking particularly at his homily on Matt 25:34–35. Perhaps only an allusion to judgment appears in our text. See Brändle, "Sweetest Passage," 127–39.

108. Clarke, *Ascetic Works of Saint Basil*, 195–96.

109. Clarke, *Ascetic Works of Saint Basil*, 214–15.

110. Sterk, *Renouncing the World*, 146.

111. The *Praktikos* is also intended for the monastic community, but Evagrius does not connect this explicitly to 2 Thessalonians. See Evagrius Ponticus, *Praktikos and Chapters on Prayer*, 18–19.

describes how this "noonday demon" afflicts the monk, but he provides a corrective firmly established in scripture, particularly 2 Thessalonians. Writing in a monastic context at this point, Cassian reminds his readers of Paul's example through manual labour, the admonition that the idle should not eat, and the proper manner of admonishing the disorderly brethren.[112] He does not, however, speak in terms of the aim of labour, like Basil, aside from its capacity to correct *acedia*. The absence of working so as to provide for the poor might be due simply to the coenobitic monasticism of Cassian, which withdrew from society where one would readily encounter the needy. The influence of Evagrius on Cassian appears in the structure and terminology of *The 12 Books*, but this does not exclude the mutual influence of Cassian and Chrysostom on each other during their time together at Constantinople. Cassian's reading of 2 Thess 3:6–15 demonstrates a number of affinities with Chrysostom.

Theodore reads 2 Thess 3:6–15 in an interesting light. Certainly, the able-bodied members must work with their hands, so as not to burden the community. At the same time, reading this passage too narrowly puts it in conflict with Paul's challenging comments to the Corinthians about the gospel worker's right to provision from the community (1 Cor 9:4–15). For this reason, Theodore contends that those engaged in teaching (i.e., priests and bishops) are free from working with their hands in a way that others are not, because they provide an essential service to the community.[113] He looks at the text from a position of a bishop who does not engage in manual labour and raises the question of how this exhortation reaches his profession. Theodore does not make a connection between work and provision for the needy. For Chrysostom, the connection is clear: *the idle* are *the poor*.[114] At the same time, Chrysostom offers a similar perspective to Theodore in a passing comment that alms are given to those who are unable to work and those who "are wholly occupied in the business of teaching."[115] Chrysostom is somehow able to realise both of these answers in the text. The difference in the social contexts (Antioch or Constantinople versus Mopsuestia) and

---

112. John Cassian, *Twelve Books* 10.7–16 (*NPNF2* 11:268–72).

113. Theodore of Mopsuestia, "In epist. ii Thess," 62–63. See also Hughes, *Constructing Antichrist*, 62–63.

114. "[Paul] is discoursing concerning the poor" (John Chrysostom, *2 Thessalonians* 5 [*NPNF1* 13:396]).

115. John Chrysostom, *2 Thessalonians* 5 (*NPNF1* 13:394).

the audience of the respective works (congregation versus educated monastics) might account for the difference in the questions posed.

With Chrysostom, John of Damascus reads this passage as referring to those who beg for food, but he quickly follows this up with the comment that they should work, after Paul's example. He then takes up a position similar to Theodore and Chrysostom in defending the right for "τοῖς τὸ Εὐαγγέλιον κηρύττουσιν" to live from the gospel (1 Cor 9:14),[116] likely eyeing his own post.

Centuries later, John Calvin exhibits the ongoing influence of the Church Father. Generally speaking, Calvin takes a harsh stance against those who do not labour, especially the monks of his day. Following Augustine in condemning idle monks, Calvin bewails their appeal to an "Order or other and sometimes with the name of some Rule" in defence of their idleness.[117] Calvin might have better excoriated them by turning the *Longer Rule* or Cassian's *12 Books* against them. Whereas the Fathers' corrections to the monastic communities stems from intimate association with them as insiders, Calvin's use of this passage comes as an outside observer.

Calvin finally engages with Chrysostom on this topic at 2 Thess 3:13. First, he cites Ambrose's opinion that "this remark has been added so that the rich should not withdraw from motives of envy the assistance which they are giving to the poor."[118] He then follows this with a similar comment from Chrysostom, who contends that the verse means a person who has been justifiably condemned as lazy should, nevertheless, not be deprived of food if they need it. Calvin argues, alternatively, that the intent of the verse is to prevent those who give generously from taking offence at the behaviour of the undeserving or those who take their generosity for granted and thereby retract the hand that gives to those in need. Here he synthesizes the perspectives of Ambrose and Chrysostom into one. These Fathers mediate the "new" voice of the Reformer.

What does not materialise in Calvin, however, is the characteristic sweetness with which Chrysostom speaks of the poor. Calvin concludes, "however the ingratitude, annoyance, pride, impertinence, and other unworthy behaviour on the part of the poor may trouble us, or discourage and disgust us, we must still strive never to abandon our desire to do good."[119]

116. John of Damascus, *In epist. ii ad Thess* (PG 95:928).
117. Calvin, *Epistles of Paul*, 419.
118. Calvin, *Epistles of Paul*, 420.
119. Calvin, *Epistles of Paul*, 420.

Chrysostom's question matures in a context in which he witnesses extreme poverty and the neglect of Christian responsibility to care for the poor. Calvin's question, alternatively, reflects a critical view of contemporary monasticism. Still, Calvin is able to envision the poor to whom Chrysostom refers, and therefore incorporates his thoughts.

On both the issues of pride and concern for the poor, it is clear how exegesis and contemporary context interact and lead to the final form of John's homilies. Pride leads to the neglect of the poor because pride is not just anti-Christ and anti-God, it is in some way anti-human. The theological impulses of his ascetic background give substance to his discussion of 2 Thessalonians and extend challenging, typically ascetic morality to the average Christian. Chrysostom's incorporation of these concerns into his reading shows how this epistle serves as an answer to his contextual questions and expand the modern horizon of understanding by grounding it practically in the experience of the Church. His reading of the "idle" as "the poor" is a unifying thread through interpretive history and that expands modern interpretations with a complementary ancient reading of the same passage.

The purpose of this section has been to show how John moves from Paul as the virtuous paragon to cultivating the virtuous Christian in the pattern of Paul. Yet, John also reveals the dark side of 2 Thessalonians: the wicked ("vicious") and Antichrist, and their place in the eschaton.

The Antichrist and his Body

Beyond the rhetorical encouragement of 2 Thessalonians, John performs two movements in his discourses about the Antichrist and pride: first, he reveals that the wicked participate in the Antichrist through the sin of pride; second, he identifies this characterizing sin of the Antichrist with the sin that caused Satan to fall.

Due to the appearance of "the man of lawlessness" in 2 Thess 2:3, whom John takes to be the Antichrist,[120] the bishop makes a connection to his own context regarding a legend about Antichrist coming "on bended

---

120. The tradition of reading the "man of lawlessness" as Antichrist was well-established by the time of Chrysostom. The beginning of this tradition can be traced *at least* as early as Irenaeus (120–202). See Irenaeus, *Against Heresies* 5.25 (*ANF* 1:553–54); McGinn, *Antichrist*, 58–60.

knees."[121] From the description in the epistle that "he will exalt himself against everything that is called god or object of worship, so as to sit in the temple of God exhibiting himself as if he is God" (2 Thess 2:4), John counters the local folklore and reveals how Antichrist is "anointed unto pride."[122] From this entry point, John demonstrates how pride is the chief of sins *in terms of origin*, stretching beyond venial sin to identification with Satan and the eschatological enemy of Christ.

The reading of this strand of apocalyptic material not only as descriptive of eschatological events, but also as a perennial problem of human conduct mirrors an approach developing simultaneously in the West through the Donatist Tyconius (d. late fourth century) and Augustine. Tyconius's *Book of Rules* exhibits a keen interest in understanding "prophetic" texts and their implications for the lives of contemporary Christians.[123] In a modified manner, Augustine appropriated the seven interpretive rules of Tyconius into his exegetical-theological enterprise,[124] which resulted in his shift to the Donatist's perspective on the Millennium.[125] His rules on "the Lord and his body" and "the devil and his body" parallel his rule on genus in species, which describes how a biblical reference to an individual entity may be an expression for its larger whole (e.g., a city within a nation) or vice-versa (e.g., Israel as a reference to the faithful within the larger nation). In this way, we can see how the pride of Antichrist applies to the members of his body.[126]

Turning his attention to Antichrist's self-exaltation "above every so-called god and every object of worship" (2 Thess 2:4), John argues that this passage does not exhibit the humility (like Paul) of Antichrist, but rather his arrogance (ἀπόνοια). Because of the clear implementation of Antichrist by Satan for his ends (2:9), John connects characteristics of the two figures:

---

121. "τοῦ κάμπτειν τὰ γόνατα" (McGinn, *Antichrist*, 470).

122. John Chrysostom, *Homilies on 2 Thess* 1 (NPNF1 13:378).

123. Tyconius's definition of "prophecy" extends broadly through the biblical literature. See Bright, *Book of Rules of Tyconius*, 9. See his preamble in Burkitt, *Book of Rules of Tyconius*, 1.

124. Augustine, *De doctrina Christiana* 3.30–37 (PL 34:16–121).

125. Augustine, *City of God* 20.7 (NPNF1 2:426–27); Backus, *Reformation Readings*, xiii–xiv.

126. In Tyconius's commentary on Revelation (extant only through later scholars) his methodology leads to a similar end, for "Antichrist ceased to be a person, but became identified with the *corpus diaboli*, the omnipresent evil, and the false Christians" (Backus, *Reformation Readings*, xiii).

"For just as the devil fell because of arrogance, so also he who is operated by him is anointed into arrogance."[127] At this juncture, Chrysostom's exegesis extends into pastoral concern, and is rooted in his ascetic-theological background in the Greek-speaking East.

The two points are intimately related, but in regards to his theological training, John takes for granted a well-developed tradition in his citation of the fall of Satan. This tradition is largely built on the interpretation of Isa 14:12–17 and Ezek 28 (esp. vv. 11–18), which describe the fall of the rulers of Babylon and Tyre, respectively. The Latin *Life of Adam and Eve* and its Greek counterpart of the same name[128] take up these biblical texts and incorporate the material into their supplemental stories to Gen 2–3.

Reading these OT texts as a description of Satan's fall continued in the Fathers with Origen, who saw the "prince of Tyre" (Ezek 28:1) and his relationship to "Eden" (28:13) as a clear indication that this was not a reference to the actual ruler of Tyre, but the "governing angel . . . set over that kingdom,"[129] whom Origen understood as Satan.[130]

Theodoret reads Ezekiel similarly, recognizing Satan as an angel who formerly had authority over Eden before his fall.[131] Crucial to these passages that shapes the patristic understanding of Satan's fall is the emphasis on the role of "pride" (Ezek 28:2, 16). It is with this history of reading that Chrysostom is able to compress the fall of Satan as due to "arrogance" (ἀπόνοια) or "pride" (ὑπερηφανία).[132] As this is the chief characteristic of the

---

127. Backus, *Reformation Readings*, xiii.

128. Believed to stem from the first century CE, Johnson contends that the two texts are based on an original Hebrew document or documents. See Charlesworth, *Old Testament Pseudepigrapha and NT*, 251. Eldridge argues, however, that one may only go so far as to suggest that the base text for the *Apocalypse* "had a Semitic character" (Eldridge, *Dying Adam*, 52–56). See also Charlesworth, *Old Testament Pseudepigrapha and NT*, 86–87. The omission of 2 Enoch is due to the uncertainty of its date. See Charlesworth, *Old Testament Pseudepigrapha*, 1:91–97.

129. Anderson, "Ezekiel 28," 135.

130. Origen, *Selecta in Ezechielem*, 28 (PG 13:820–21). See also Origen, *De Principiis* 1.5.4–5 (ANF 4:258–60); Tertullian, *Against Marcion* 2.10 (ANF 3:306); Bell, *Deliver Us from Evil*, 12–13, 19.

131. Anderson, "Ezekiel 28," 138; Theodoret, *In Ezechielis* (PG 81:1093).

132. Chrysostom unifies and distinguishes these terms. The Antichrist openly exhibits ἀπόνοια, which is the "beginning of sin" in terms of foundation, namely that it sustains sin. At the same time Chrysostom cautions against ὑπερηφανία, which is the "beginning of sin" in terms of first impulse. The latter leads to the former. See John Chrysostom, *In epist. ii ad Thess* 1 (PG 62:470–1).

The Early Church

devil, Chrysostom easily applies the trait to the one through whom Satan will work as the *eschaton* approaches (2 Thess 2:9) and who mimics the behaviour described in Isa 14 and Ezek 28.

The attention to pride certainly grows out of John's observation of Antichrist's behaviour as well as the abundance of contrast between pride and humility in the OT, yet his historical context also primes him to notice this characteristic. In the same century as Chrysostom, for example, Pseudo-Hippolytus references this particular passage and describes Antichrist as "lifted up in heart" and "haughty."[133]

Additionally, numerous Fathers wrote on the vice of pride around the time of Chrysostom. In his ascetic works, Basil of Caesarea describes how the monastic community is to deal with the proud and the idle,[134] thus making an implicit connection to 2 Thessalonians. More significant, however, might be the work of the Syrian Pseudo-Macarius, who exemplifies well the theology of Syrian monasticism, in which Chrysostom had trained. In his spiritual homilies, dating to the 380s,[135] Pseudo-Macarius comments frequently on pride, at one point observing, "A proud mind is a great humiliation, while humility is a great uplifting of the mind and an honor and a dignity."[136] Like Chrysostom, he advances humility in place of pride.[137] Elsewhere, Pseudo-Macarius includes "pride" and "vainglory" in his list of vices,[138] and he issues a warning on the danger of pride in causing one to "fall away."[139]

Around the same time as Pseudo-Marcarius, Evagrius Ponticus composed his *Praktikos* in Egypt. Evagrius was raised near Antioch in the region of Pontus and heavily influenced by the Cappadocians, who trained

---

133. "ὑψοῦται τῇ καρδίᾳ" and "ὑψηλός," respectively; the former follows the Hebrew expression מוּר בְּבָל. See Pseudo-Hippolytus, *Oratio S. Hippolyti* 25 (PG 10:928).

134. Clarke, *Ascetic Works of Saint Basil*, 195–96. Basil's connection to Chrysostom should not be underestimated. This Cappadocian Father studied with Diodore in Athens and maintained contact with his friend. See Basil of Caesarea, *Letters* 134; Chase, *Chrysostom*, 10–11.

135. Maloney, *Pseudo-Macarius*, xii.

136. Maloney, *Pseudo-Macarius*, 149.

137. John Chrysostom, *In epist. ii ad Thess* 1 (PG 62:470–71).

138. Maloney, *Pseudo-Macarius*, 214.

139. Maloney, *Pseudo-Macarius*, 249–52, 259–60. It is likely, in fact, that Pseudo-Macarius influenced Gregory of Nyssa, and that *De Institutio Christiano* is a reworking of the *Great Letter*, which would have further disseminated his teachings on vices and virtues.

him and encouraged his monastic lifestyle.[140] He settled in the Nitrian desert of Egypt, where numerous other monks, including John Cassian, would come under his theological influence.[141] The *Praktikos* significantly formed the foundation for the later-developed "seven deadly sins." In the *Praktikos*, Evagrius describes the eight passionate *logismoi* in relation to monasticism. He concludes with pride as "the cause of the most damaging fall for the soul," which is quickly followed by a number of other vices and demons.[142]

Evagrius has a discernable effect on his student, Cassian, who assembles a list of the same eight passionate thoughts (though he switches the order of "sadness" and "anger"), which concludes with "pride" (ὑπερηφανία) as the most serious principle fault.[143] Cassian expounds a great deal on pride, even carrying forward the tradition that Lucifer, the archangel, fell by pride and became Satan.[144] Thus, Cassian shares the sentiment that the presence of pride in an individual is identification with the devil. In the case of Cassian, it is likely that primarily Evagrius influenced his understanding of pride, but John surely sharpened his views during his time at Constantinople.[145]

At first it may seem that John's view of pride may have been distilled through Pseudo-Macarius and Evagrius Ponticus. Yet, Chrysostom exhibits incipient thoughts on this topic in his letter to Theodore (368 CE).[146] This is not to say that Pseudo-Macarius or Evagrius did not hone his thoughts on the topic, but that the sensitivity to this vice was ubiquitous in ascetic circles in the East during the time of Chrysostom prior to the writings of these Fathers. It is likely that Chrysostom would have come into contact with Evagrius's work at Constantinople, either through the preserved text or through Cassian. The sharpening of ascetic-moralism, both in terms

---

140. For an example of Evagrius's theological relationship to the Cappadocians, see Corrigan, *Evagrius and Basil*; Casiday, *Evagrius Ponticus*, 6–7.

141. Evagrius Ponticus, *Praktikos and Chapters on Prayer*, xxxv–xlviii.

142. Evagrius Ponticus, *Praktikos and Chapters on Prayer*, 20. A precedent for these vices appears in *T. Benjamin* 7.2 as the ἑπτά κακῶν. Interestingly, the text also references Beliar. See also *T. Reuben* 2.1–9, for a list of "seven spirits of deceit."

143. "Although it is the latest in our conflict with our faults and stands last on the list, yet in the order of time is the first" (John Cassian, *Twelve Books* 12.1 [NPNF2 11:280]).

144. John Cassian, *Twelve Books* 12.4 (NPNF2 11:280).

145. After the Anthropomorphite controversy, Cassian sought refuge under Chrysostom, who eventually ordained Cassian, at Constantinople. See Goodrich, *Contextualizing Cassian*, 3.

146. John Chrysostom, *Ad Theodorum lapsum I* (PG 47:277–308).

of recognizing the vice of pride and "extirpating"[147] it by humility, would then have been mutual in this regard.[148] Furthermore, the influence of the canonical dialogue on "pride and humility" played an instrumental role in the theology of Judaism and the early Church, including the monastic movements. Even in the West, Augustine begins *Confessions* with a comment about humanity and God "resisting the proud" (1 Pet 5:5).[149]

Assuming John's stance toward pride is a product of his context, the sermon of Severian following Chrysostom's first exile is decidedly antagonistic. He argues, "[John's] boastful disposition" (τὸ ἀλιζονικὸν ἦθος αὐτοῦ) alone justified his deposition and followed this with the quote "God opposes the proud (ὑπερηφάνοις)" (James 4:6; 1 Pet 5:5).[150] Whether we accept the historicity of Socrates's account of this sermon or not, the historical context would justify the degree of outrage experienced by the (hypothetical) audience. Severian describes John as characterised by the very sin that he taught to be most deplorable.

In the broader history of reception we see the immediate influence of John on Calvin's reading of the Antichrist's self-exaltation. Calvin possessed a copy of Chrysostom's homilies and relied primarily on Chrysostom for exegetical guidance above Augustine.[151] When looking at the description of Antichrist as one who exalts himself over every object of worship and god, etc. (2 Thess 2:4), Calvin notes, "the pride and arrogance of Antichrist will be so great that he raises himself above the rank and number of the servants, and mounts the throne of God with intolerable pride."[152] Significantly, Calvin notes both the *pride* and *arrogance* of Antichrist—the same terms as John in his first homily on the epistle. Calvin's reading, however, is not grounded in the context of ascetic-morality of the fourth century, nor does he contrast it with the virtue of humility.

---

147. John Chrysostom, *2 Thessalonians* 1 (*NPNF1* 13:378).
148. John Cassian, *Twelve Books* 12.8 (*NPNF2* 11:282).
149. Augustine, *Confessions*, 3.
150. Socrates Scholasticus, *Historia Ecclesiastica* 6.16 (PG 67:714).
151. Walchenbach, *Calvin as Biblical Commentator*, 1–43.
152. According to the French edition: "*L'orguiel et arrogance* de l'Antichrist sera si grande" (Calvin, *Commentaires de Jehan Calvin*, 164). The Latin edition notes only "pride" (*superbia*), which is still the same terminology found in the Latin edition of Chrysostom. See Calvin, *Iohannis Calvini*, 210; John Chrysostom, *In epist. ii ad Thess* 1 (PG 62:470).

Turning to modern commentators on this same verse and topic, we observe similar attention to the pride of Antichrist in Rigaux.[153] In 2 Thess 2:4, he sees Paul characterizes Antichrist by "une opposition *orgueilleuse* à tout ce qui est divin ou sacré. . . . Impie, *orgueilleux*, blasphémateur, tels sont les traits qui stigmatisent l'horrible figure."[154] Rigaux shows further that one can trace the opposition and pride against the sacred found here to Dan 11:36.[155] This reveals the textual relationship of our passage to the OT, which Chrysostom does not insinuate. In addition to this, Rigaux situates 2 Thessalonians further in the apocalyptic genre by way of comparison with other apocalyptic texts.

Wanamaker follows Rigaux in this regard, commenting on the relationship of the passage to Dan 11:36 as a description of Antiochus Epiphanes. He adds that in the tradition out of which 2 Thess 2:4 originated "the arrogance of the person of rebellion . . . would culminate or result in his usurpation of the temple of God to declare his own divinity."[156] He extends the argument further by connecting the passage to Ezek 28:1–10 and Isa 14:4–20, in which historical rulers arrogated to themselves the claim of divinity.[157] In Chrysostom's day, these passages were understood as a description of Satan's fall, and served as the loaded background behind Chrysostom's statement "Satan fell by arrogance."[158] Wanamaker does not assume such a connection, but continues by grounding 2 Thessalonians in a context of religious-political turmoil, in which the pride of Caligula conflicted with the beliefs of the early Christians. This ruler recapitulated Daniel's prophecy and served as a contemporary type for the future eschatological enemy of Christ. Through such rulers, the mystery of lawlessness continues to work, Wanamaker contends. He adds further that modern Christians face similar, yet more complex problems, such as nations and political figures arrogating to themselves "Christian symbols to legitimate their unjust and oppressive practices such as apartheid, militarism, and

---

153. Rigaux refers to the "man of lawlessness" as "anti-Dieu" rather than "Antéchrist" (Rigaux, *Thessaloniciens*, 658).

154. Rigaux, *Thessaloniciens*, 658 (emphasis added).

155. Rigaux, *Thessaloniciens*, 658.

156. Wanamaker, *Thessalonians*, 246.

157. Wanamaker, *Thessalonians*, 247–48.

158. John Chrysostom, *In epist. ii ad Thess* 1 (PG 62:470).

imperialism."[159] Wanamaker offers a pastoral reflection of the same tone as Chrysostom but locates the attention in a different place.

The history of interpretation shows that readers have understood the activity of Antichrist in terms of arrogance and pride, yet for Chrysostom these terms are couched in an inherited tradition regarding the fall of Satan and an ascetic-moralism that developed out of this tradition. His reading becomes introspective and provides correction, "satisfying" the original horizon of expectations, but his censure of pride has lost its sharpness in the progress of history. Rigaux's exegesis situates the letter in a literary and political context, which Wanamaker utilizes to turn the gaze of Christians outward, that they might become aware of Antichrist-arrogance, systemic sin, exhibited by leaders or nations in the present and stand against it (though he does not specify how). These complementary readings, when taken together, generate a horizon of understanding pride and Antichrist in the world that is denser than any of the readings taken individually. The text is not simply about an eschatological event, but it is also about the manifestation of and identification with this eschatological figure *against* God in the present.

CONCLUSION

In summary, we see how multiple influences culminate in John's particular reading of 2 Thessalonians. His Antiochene exegetical heritage, rhetorical training, admiration for Paul, pastoral post, and ascetic-moralism come together in service of his ascetic-theological reading of 2 Thessalonians, which are subsumed under the biblical rhetoric of "the proud and the humble," which features throughout the OT, especially in the Psalms and Sirach, but takes on an eschatological tone in the NT. In the interpretive process, John displays practical concern for his hearers. His voice sounds at home amongst the Eastern Fathers, yet his epochal reading registers aesthetically valuable in particular instances and especially in how he structures his reading along the lines of virtue and vice. From here, we venture west to ninth-century France.

---

159. Wanamaker, *Thessalonians*, 248–49.

3

The Medieval Church
Haimo of Auxerre

BACKGROUND

AROUND THE TURN OF the twentieth century, Riggenbach's rediscovery of Haimo of Auxerre[1] lifted him from the fog of the historical past and revealed that the bulk of his works were erroneously attributed to Haymo of Halberstadt (d. 853) or Remigius of Auxerre (d. 908).[2] Haimo arrived in the wake of the Carolingian reforms, which saw the shift of learning centres from the British Isles to the Continent and the "upgrading of the intellectual qualifications of the clergy, both monastic and secular."[3] Of primary importance was education as preparation for the study of scriptures, which entailed engagement with the Fathers and the Bible as inseparable authorities.

The details of Haimo's origins are unclear,[4] though he certainly flourished during the Carolingian era at the Abbey of St. Germain in Auxerre,

---

1. Riggenbach, *Die ältesten lateinischen Kommentare*.

2. For a more complete list of false attributions, see Heil, "Haimo's Commentary," 112–13.

3. Colish, *Medieval Foundations*, 66.

4. Heil suggests Spain as Haimo's place of birth because of, among other points, his eventual relocation to Cessy-les-Bois, which was populated at the time by Spanish

in modern-day France, and the bulk of his work came from 840–860.[5] Haimo appears shortly after the significant work of Bede and the Irish scholars, and was himself educated by the Irish master Murethach.[6]

As a commentator, Haimo contributes innovative, exegetical insights, which accounts for the widespread influence of his works in the generations that followed. Such distinction from his predecessors garners only a nod from Beryl Smalley, who says, "Haimo stands on the line that divides the compiler of select extracts from the author of a commentary," yet he is still bound by tradition and lacks the sophistication of John Scottus Eriugena.[7] As research on Haimo progresses, though, and more works authored by Haimo are uncovered, scholars are put in a position of having to recognize the significance and unique contributions of this obscure monk.[8]

Evidence of a sermon on 1 John 5:4–10 from the abbot Haimo of Cessy-les-Bois indicates that Haimo was transferred to this abbey from St. Germain later in his life. He likely died sometime between 875 and 878.[9]

---

emigrants, and his apparent alignment with the approach of Theodulf of Orléans over against the insular "exegesis and tradition" adopted by Alcuin and Rabanus Maurus. See Heil, "Haimo's Commentary," 114–19.

5. Riggenbach, *Die ältesten lateinischen Kommentare*, 80; Smalley, *Study of the Bible*, 39; Contreni, "Haimo of Auxerre," 310; Holtz, "Introduction," xxiv; Hughes, *Constructing Antichrist*, 146.

6. Holtz, "Introduction," xxix–xxxi, xxxiii–xxxiv; Contreni has challenged this stance insofar as it places Murethach and Haimo in a teacher-student relationship. He suggests instead that they were colleagues in the 830s (Contreni, "By Lions," 54). Heil follows Contreni in this regard, arguing further that Theodulf of Orléans was a key theological influence on Haimo (Heil, "Theodulf," 118–20).

7. Smalley, *Study of the Bible*, 39–40.

8. Heil goes so far as to describe Haimo as the "Höhepunkt der karolingischen Exegese" (Heil, *Kompilation oder Konstruktion?*, 275). Swanson challenges Smalley's argument by including Haimo along with John Scottus as two of the "more original scholars of the ninth century" who move beyond simply listing sources to renewing the "tradition of scholarly comment" (Swanson, "Glossa Ordinaria," 161). Matter locates Smalley's failure to give Haimo higher consideration in her primary interest in the "literal sense of the biblical text" (Matter, "Haimo's Commentary," 49–90).

9. Contreni, "Abbot of Sasceium," 311–17. It is possible that Haimo left for Cessy-les-Bois in the 850s. See Contreni, "By Lions," 52–56; Quadri, "Aimone di Auxerre," 17–18.

Diachrony and The Synchronic Canon

Haimo followed on the heels of several well-known scholars—Bede, Alcuin, Claudius of Turin, Smaragdus of Saint-Mihiel, and Admonán[10]—and he engaged with each of these scholars in some capacity. Following the exegetical standards set by these predecessors, Haimo relied heavily on the Church Fathers in his work, but particularly in his commentaries. Where he differs from these scholars and his contemporaries (e.g., Rabanus Maurus, Paschasius Radbertus, and Florus of Lyon), however, is in his ability to seamlessly synthesise and summarise the Fathers, rather than simply quote them in large blocks of text on a given biblical passage.

The influence of Haimo extends in the immediate generations following him to scholars such as Heiric of Auxerre (his student), Remigius of Auxerre (student of Heiric), Ælfric of Eynsham, Adso of Montier-en-Der, Peter Lombard, and even Aquinas and Bonaventure. In the case of the former three, Haimo's importance is reflected primarily in his appearance beside the Church Fathers in their homilaries.[11] Similarly, the incorporation of Haimo in the various *Glossae* in circulation demonstrates the influential nature of this scholar's work.[12]

2 Thessalonians Commentary: Provenance, Audience, and Structure

As the most widely-disseminated of his works,[13] Haimo's commentary on Paul played an important role in medieval exegesis of the apostle's letters. The limited scope of our research focuses on Haimo's interaction with 2 Thessalonians from this volume, but also gives occasional attention to his incorporation of 2 Thessalonians into his homilies and *florilegia*. All of

---

10. The hermeneutical influence of Admonán via Murethach is more abundantly clear in Haimo's other works, including the commentary on 1 Thessalonians. See O'Loughlin, "*Res, tempus, locus, persona*," 139–58.

11. Barré, *Les homéliaires carolingiens*; Ælfric of Eynsham, *Aelfric's Catholic Homilies*, liv–lv.

12. The significance of Haimo in this regard is exemplified in the Rusch Glossa, in which Haimo, Augustine, and Jerome are the only cited authorities on 2 Thessalonians. See Rusch, *Biblia cum glossa ordinaria*, 400–404.

13. Iogna-Prat has tabulated a total of 166 extant manuscripts of Haimo's Pauline commentary dating up to the end of the fifteenth century. See Iogna-Prat, "L'œuvre d'Haymon d'Auxerre," 161.

these sources were likely composed during his time in Auxerre and disseminated by his students, who departed before his relocation.

The great range of influence that Haimo's work on 2 Thessalonians held in the Middle Ages as the transitional link between patristic scholarship and the High Middle Ages is the reason for its selection as an epochal moment in the history of the epistle.[14] He initiated a trajectory for hearing 2 Thessalonians in a particular manner and therefore accounts for the influence of his minimally-apocalyptic reading over against, for example, the contemporary work of Thietland of Einsiedeln.

As with all of his Pauline commentaries, Haimo introduces the letter with an *argumentum*[15] and proceeds to comment on select, consecutive lemmas. Theologically, this commentary represents a strand of what Hughes terms "apocalyptic realism," which understands Antichrist as "*imminent* and *external*" and 2 Thessalonians generally as a prophetic timeline of future events.[16] Haimo tends toward a more literal reading of Paul, yet fully adopts a Tyconian-Augustinian approach toward Revelation. This spiritual, or "actualizing," reading of Revelation allows the imagery of the text to be understood as correlative to the reader's present and perennial theological issues without restricting it to a single historical person or event.[17] Such interpretation has its roots in the seven interpretive keys of Tyconius discussed in the previous chapter. Haimo's Revelation commentary also differs from his 2 Thessalonians commentary by beginning with a *praefatio*, which introduces the setting in which John authored the book and details the nature of prophecy without describing the content or argument of Revelation.

Differing from the commentators of his time who either repeat in full the works of the Fathers or offer a selection of excerpts on the biblical book under investigation, Haimo's commentaries recapture something of the style of the Church Fathers. His audience is likely an eclectic group of monks, scholars, and laity, with the commentary designed to faithfully

---

14. For a substantiation of this position, see Hughes, *Constructing Antichrist*, 126, 146–51.

15. The only exception in the Migne text is the Colossians commentary, but the absence of the *argumentum* might be attributed to a poor manuscript source. The Migne Colossians text, unlike 2 Thessalonians, has a number of omissions when compared with extant manuscripts of Haimo's Pauline corpus. See Hughes, *Constructing Antichrist*, 150.

16. Hughes, *Constructing Antichrist*, 23, 165, 243.

17. Kovacs and Rowland, *Revelation*, 9.

bring together patristic material, offer new insights, and provide content for sermons.

Using the Vulgate text of 2 Thessalonians, Haimo opens his commentary with an *argumentum*, which summarizes his understanding of the epistle as the Apostle's response to the Thessalonians' fear that they would be condemned because of a misunderstanding of the content of the First Epistle. In 2 Thessalonians, Paul offers an eschatological timeline to reassure the Thessalonian church. Haimo follows the *argumentum* with commentary on all three chapters of the epistle, with attention dedicated only to selected lemmas, rather than every verse. Haimo follows Paul's purpose literally and pastorally.

On the first five verses of the book, he discusses the growth of faith and the providential nature of tribulation and judgment. Of the remaining verses of 2 Thess 1, Haimo (like Chrysostom) emphasizes the causal force of *si tamen*, the physical nature of Christ's judgment with fire, the mutual "giving" of eternal punishment by the reprobate, and the reception of the gospel by the Thessalonians.

The bulk of his commentary concentrates on the second chapter of 2 Thessalonians, which Haimo believes to be a description of Christ's Second-Coming and the apocalyptic events that must precede it. The "apostasy" (2:3) he recognizes as the desertion of all kingdoms from Roman rule, which has already taken place. Rome was "what restrains" (*quid detineat*; 2:6) the arrival of Antichrist, but is no longer in place. Therefore, his arrival is only now restricted by the providence of God. The "man of sin" (i.e., Antichrist; 2:3), who is the imitative son of Satan, indwelt by the fullness of iniquity, and the inverse image of Christ, is yet to come and may either install himself in the Jerusalem Temple, or in the Church. The "mystery of iniquity already at work" (2:7) is the persecution of the Church from Nero to Diocletian, and then again with Julian. These are the members of Antichrist as the faithful are members of Christ. It follows in this paradigm that "he who now holds" (*ut qui tenet nunc*; 2:7) is the Roman emperor, as the specific manifestation of the kingdom's power. When the kingdom falls, Antichrist will arrive by the work of Satan, establishing his throne on the Mount of Olives and performing false miracles akin to those of Simon Magus, deceiving the reprobate under the permission of God (2:9–11). Either Christ or Michael will destroy Antichrist (2:8). Therefore, the readers are to be consoled through the past gift of Christ's life in divine love and the expectation of the future kingdom (2:16–17).

Haimo offers the least material on the final chapter of the epistle, amounting to less that half a column in the Migne text. Of note is his exegesis of the variant readings *patientia Christi* (3:5), as patience in persecution, and *exspectatione Christi*, as awaiting the arrival of Christ, without suggesting which variant is correct. Interestingly, Haimo virtually omits any discussion of Church discipline for the "busybodies," which is the section of chapter 3 that has received the most attention historically.[18] He adds only that people must labour for their food, or else they should be brought to "our" (*nos*) attention for the purpose of rebuking. He concludes by appropriating the closing grace (3:18) of the letter as his own for his reader by offering only the Vulgate text without comment.

Influential Impulses for Interpreting 2 Thessalonians

Regarding the influential impulses that shape Haimo's reception of 2 Thessalonians, it is important to offer a preliminary note on his relationship to the Fathers, and Augustine in particular. The value of the Fathers to the Carolingians is not without precedent. The influential scholars of the British Isles who came before them established an exegetical trend in utilizing the Fathers that most would follow. For all the ingenuity that Bede, as an example, exhibits in his *Historia Ecclesiastica*, his commentary on Paul simply listing large blocks of text by Augustine on given passages of scripture. Not laziness, but respect for Augustine motivates this approach to commenting.

In the case of 2 Thessalonians, Bede comments only on 2:1–12 and 3:14 by way of *City of God* 20.13 and Augustine's treatise on Psalm 100.[19] The English designation of Bede's work on the Pauline corpus as "excerpts" rather than as a commentary is more appropriate, as it does not engage immediately with the epistle, nor does it comment on its entirety. Nevertheless,

---

18. This omission is conspicuous and likely indicates two, interrelated points: the commentary on 2 Thessalonians was originally a sermon for laity (and made into a commentary for monks and clerics as a preaching aide), and, as a Benedictine monk, Haimo was under the Rule of St. Benedict, which reads 2 Thess 3 as a warning to the idle and busybodies in the monastic community. For a common, contemporary perspective in this regard, Smaragdus's commentary on the Rule of St. Benedict also takes up the monastic command to work, as read through the lens of 2 Thess 3. See Smaragdus Abbas, *Commentaria in regulam Sancti Benedicti* (PL 102:884–87). The suggestion that Haimo distinguished between the laity and clergy resonates with Ortigues perspective that Haimo was a theorist of the "three orders" (clergy, nobility, and the third estate) of Christian society (Ortigues, "L'élaboration de la théorie," 29–43).

19. Bede, *Saint Augustine*, 291–94.

Bede serves as a representative of the biblical commentator's mind in the time leading up to and during much of the Carolingian era.

Haimo's contemporary, Florus of Lyon (d. 860), demonstrates an incredibly similar approach to Bede. Though he dedicates more attention to the fullness of 2 Thessalonians, his work amounts to an index of Augustine's works in which particular verses to 2 Thessalonians appear. He likewise does not comment on the 2 Thessalonians itself.[20]

In several respects, then, Haimo differs from his predecessors and contemporaries. Like Bede and Florus, Haimo generally relies heavily on Augustine, but he also gives great weight to the interpretations of Gregory the Great, Jerome, and Ambrosiaster.[21] The former three were highly significant authorities for the majority of medieval interpreters, yet Ambrosiaster tends to dominate Haimo's reading of the Pauline epistles.

Additionally, Haimo does not list large blocks of text from the Fathers, but tends to summarise and combine their thoughts in his own words without always citing the source upon which he relies. At times, he frequently combines differing views from amongst the Fathers on a passage without attempting to resolve the conflict, thereby respecting their authority and not going beyond permissible exegetical limits for a Carolingian monk.[22] The tradition of citing large portions of patristic authorities on a biblical text continues after the death of Haimo in the *Glossa Ordinaria*. This contextually distinctive approach to commentary construction resembles a patristic model. Thus Haimo provokes his horizon by reviving in part a historic form of commentary genre, yet he remains distinct by seamlessly blending his authoritative sources, without necessarily having to cite them. The unanswerable question has to do with whether Haimo wrote in this

---

20. Florus of Lyon, *In epist. ii ad Thess* (PL 119:397–398). Though not available in Migne, Florus compiled similar indices of Jerome and Gregory. See Fransen, "Hiéronymienne de Florus," 195–228; "Grégorienne de Florus," 278–317.

21. Augustine, Gregory, Jerome, and Ambrose were the "four great fathers" of medieval exegesis. Haimo's primary reliance on Ambrosiaster alongside the former three throughout his Pauline commentary is indicative of the medieval ascription of Ambrosiaster's commentary to Ambrose. See Hughes, *Constructing Antichrist*, 123. To a lesser extent, Haimo used Origen, Chrysostom, Cassian, Cassiodor, Cyprian of Carthage, Ephraem, and Hilary of Poitiers. See Heil, "Haimo's Commentary," 109.

22. Hughes, "Haimo of Auxerre," 15–16. See also Contreni, "Haimo of Auxerre's Commentary," 231. The limits of interpretation are set well by the Vincentian Canon as that which has been held "everywhere, always, and by all"—thus restricting "new" interpretations without reference to the Fathers. See Goering, "Introduction," 198.

manner for emulatory purposes, or whether he considered his own position as authoritative (or both).

Other contemporaries who composed commentaries on 2 Thessalonians include Rabanus Maurus, Claude of Turin, and Sedulius Scottus. Rabanus refers to Augustine explicitly once, but cites a number of other Fathers, especially Theodore of Mopsuestia, who provides the structure for his commentary and whom he cites as "Ambrose."[23] These commentaries are all eschatological in tone.

Against the developed tradition of relating Augustine in any way possible to a biblical text,[24] Haimo only indirectly incorporates Augustine in his 2 Thessalonians commentary. On 2 Thess 1:4 Haimo cites Prosper, the authorised interpreter of Augustine, to elaborate on the sovereignty of God. Given the structure of his commentary, Haimo's work is something of a shock to the horizon of expectations of his first readers. The freedom of format should have seen the inclusion of Augustine.

The reason for this omission lies in Haimo's *argumentum* for the epistle. The Carolingian recognizes the letter as a "thorough summary of the historical events and characters of the end, complete with an analysis of the theological issues that pertain to them."[25] Augustine is hesitant to assert such definitive statements about a text that remains obscure on details like the identity of the Restrainer and the man of lawlessness. Eventually, Augustine settles on a spiritual reading of 2 Thessalonians that sees the text articulating the activity of "Antichrist" at present in the Church and he dismisses overly-eschatological readings of the passage.[26]

In a context/tradition that has been shaped to read this passage eschatologically, Haimo faces a difficulty with Augustine. Rather than disagree openly with him, however, Haimo pursues a wiser route of omission and

---

23. Hughes, "Augustine and Adversary," 228. Rabanus also makes use of Cassian, Jerome, and Gregory the Great. See Rabanus Maurus, *Exposito in epist. ii ad Thess* (PL 112:565–80).

24. "Early Medieval exegetes revered the authority of Augustine, and few if any dared to challenge him directly. So great was Augustine's authority that the great doctrinal debates of the early Middle Ages—for example, the debate over predestination—were never understood to be for or against Augustine, but rather over those whose interpretation of Augustine was correct" (Hughes, *Constructing Antichrist*, 115–16).

25. Hughes, "Augustine and Adversary," 230.

26. Hughes, *Constructing Antichrist*, 194–208, esp. 206–8; "Augustine and Adversary," 223–26.

garnering patristic support from elsewhere, namely in the perspectives of Jerome, Gregory, and Ambrosiaster on the epistle.[27]

Yet Haimo's reading is not prohibitively restricted by the Fathers, and it is because of this that he can focus on what he perceives to be the primary function of this epistle (and of his own composition): rejecting heresy and false doctrine. Unlike Chrysostom, who recognizes this purpose, but focuses pastorally on the cultivation of the virtuous Christian, Haimo attends to this theme throughout his exegesis. For this reason, we look at the four areas of heresy and false doctrine that capture his attention: predestination, simony, apocalyptic realism, and millenarianism. The former two topics are more isolated in their occurrences and receive attention first, while the latter Haimo treats more persistently throughout his reading of the epistle.

AGAINST HERESIES

Double- or Single-Predestination

Heresies, particularly historically distant heresies, feature prominently in Haimo's works. Riggenbach even goes so far as to contend that defence against heresy is one of Haimo's primary concerns throughout his work.[28] In the first example of this commentary, Haimo takes a position toward predestination that follows on the controversy between Gottschalk of Orbais (d. 867) and Hincmar of Reims (d. 882).

Gottschalk's career began in the monastery of Fulda under the watchful eye of the abbot, Rabanus Maurus. After coming of age, Gottschalk sought and succeeded in gaining freedom from monasticism at the synod of Mainz (829). His abbot, Rabanus had attempted to constrain his bright pupil by accusing him of heresy with regard to his teaching on double-predestination, but was unsuccessful. Having travelled and taught extensively, primarily in Orbais and Corbie, Gottschalk found numerous allies to his position, such as Servatus Lupus, in which he maintained that God predestined *both* the elect to salvation *and* the reprobate to damnation,

---

27. This omission is rendered starker by Haimo's heavy use of Augustine in his commentaries on Romans–2 Corinthians.

28. Riggenbach, *Die ältesten lateinischen Kommentare*, 69. For the heresies castigated by Haimo, see Contreni, "Abbot of Sasceium," 309; Quadri, "Aimone Di Auxerre."

The Medieval Church

expounding this doctrine from the teaching of Augustine, who is, admittedly, a major contributor to this dispute and a cause of the confusion.[29]

Rabanus, who held the orthodox view of single-predestination, marshalled the support of Gottschalk's primary opponent: Hincmar of Reims. The debate between the groups lasted for years and led to further doctrinal considerations for generations to come, namely with regard to the topics of atonement and the authority of the Fathers, particularly Augustine.[30] The debate circulated around the interrelation of grace, free-will, foreknowledge, and predestination as articulated by Augustine and eventually came out in favour of Hincmar and Rabanus, who had Gottschalk's position condemned at the Councils of Quiercy (853) and Valence (855), and a synod at Langres (859).[31]

In this climate, Haimo enters a veritable minefield by commenting on a biblical text that makes frequent reference to the salvation of the saints and the condemnation of the wicked. The debate shapes his reading of 2 Thessalonians and he tows the orthodox line in the tone of Hincmar. Furthermore, Haimo arrives during a shift in the tradition from a focus on predestination and free-will to *whom God predestines.*

In his opening comments on the epistle, Haimo observes that the tribulations endured by the Thessalonians are "an example of the just judgment of God" (1:5). He qualifies this with an observation from Prosper: nothing happens unless God permits it. Thus God *allows* the saints to suffer as an indication of the greater degree of judgment that the wicked will endure for inflicting the elect.[32] Predestination relates primarily to salvation, but the suffering of the righteous does not preclude his sovereignty.

In the Lord's arrival in "flaming fire" to judge the reprobate (1:8), Haimo comments that the fire will simultaneously "purify the elect,"[33] and sweep the wicked into hell. At the beginning of chapter 2, he calls the elect those "gathering" (2:1) to the Lord at his advent.[34] Lastly, as the chapter

---

29. Otten, "Carolingian Theology," 77.

30. For further discussion on the nature and arguments levelled in this debate, see Pelikan, *Christian Tradition*, 3:80–95.

31. Pelikan, *Christian Tradition*, 3:93–94.

32. Haimo of Auxerre, *In epist. ii ad Thess* (PL 117:778).

33. "[Flamma] purgabit electos" (Haimo of Auxerre, *In epist. ii ad Thess* [PL 117:778–79]). The fact that Haimo uses language of "the elect" in this discussion despite its absence from the epistle situates it more firmly in the context of the broader debate on predestination.

34. Though he follows this with the point "either that crowd which will come with

draws to a close, Haimo observes that God's sending the perishing a "work of error" (2:11) means that God will *permit* Antichrist to come to them and deceive them. In this way, their condemnation comes about by their free choice to reject "the love of truth" and to follow Antichrist instead.[35]

Nowhere does Haimo refer to the predestination of the wicked to condemnation, only the certainty that they will suffer, which falls under divine foreknowledge rather than predestination.[36] Additionally, Haimo only speaks of *the elect* as those being *preveniently-appointed* to an eternal outcome. With relation to the entirety of 2 Thessalonians, Haimo introduces a new aspect to its history from his ecclesial milieu in clarifying the dimensions of predestination and the permissive sovereignty of God.

In the centuries that follow, Aquinas will offer an important clarification on the idea of predestination with regard to first and efficient causes, and John Calvin will return the discussion to double-predestination. The reception history of "predestination" could fill volumes that ultimately distract from the goal of our particular project. It is sufficient here to locate Haimo in his diachronic and synchronic canons, and to highlight his contribution to satisfying the horizon of expectations.

Simony

The second, and more specific reference to heresy in Haimo's commentary is the seemingly off-hand comment about the historically distant Simon Magus. The inclusion of this character from Acts 8:9–24 in the commentary appears to offer little more than an example of how he reflects characteristics similar to the Antichrist by performing lying signs and miracles (2:9). In describing Antichrist, Haimo remarks, "he will appear to resurrect the dead and do many other signs, but these are lies and foreign to the truth since he will delude men through magical art and illusion, just as Simon Magus deceived the one who, thinking he was killing Simon, beheaded a

---

him or which will meet with him for judgment," this refers to the idea of "gathering" rather than election. He clarifies this by adding "all the elect are in Christ, as members joined to him"—a point he certainly would not make about the reprobate (Haimo of Auxerre, "Exposition," 24).

35. Haimo of Auxerre, *In epist. ii ad Thess* (PL 117:782).

36. Hincmar draws this distinction against the work of Gottschalk. See Pelikan, *Christian Tradition*, 3:86.

ram in his place."[37] This attention to Simon's act of subterfuge by substituting a ram for himself makes clear that Haimo has a more developed, apocryphal understanding of the heretic.

In the centuries leading up to Haimo, the heresy of simony, or paying for a clerical position, was rife in the Christian world. At the Council of Chalcedon (451), simony received sole attention in the second canon and was condemned as heretical.[38] Gregory the Great went to extensive lengths to reform the Church in this regard, particularly in the areas of the world that seemed just beyond papal reach, such as Austrasia and Burgundy. For this reason, he frequently wrote to the queen of these regions, Brunhild,[39] layering flattery with requests that she strive to stamp out simony from her kingdom, though his attempts never matured into the council for which he had hoped.[40] In his works, Gregory articulated three types of simony: payment for a clerical office in money, payment of the same in esteem/flattery, and complacency in the perpetuation of simony when one has the power to stop it.[41]

---

37. Haimo of Auxerre, "Exposition," 29. Simon also appears in Haimo's Philippians commentary in a misquote of Jerome about his claim to be the son of God and the Paraclete (PL 117:740; cf. Jerome, *Commentarius in Matthaeum* 24.5 [PL 26:176]), in his 1 Timothy commentary as an example alongside Hymenaeus and Alexander of one who "fell away" (PL 117:788), and his Apocalypse commentary as a predecessor to the dragon and beast in the way that he performs false miracles (PL 117:1133; cf. Rev 16:14).

38. "If any Bishop should ordain for money, and put to sale a grace which cannot be sold ... let him who is convicted of this forfeit his own rank.... And if any one should be found negotiating such shameful and unlawful transactions, let him also, if he is a clergyman, be deposed from his rank, and if he is a layman or monk, let him be anathematized" (*XXX Canons* [NNPF2 14:268-69]). A briefer form of this condemnation appears earlier in the apocryphal work *The Apostolic Constitutions* on the lips of Peter: "If any bishop obtains that dignity by money, or even a presbyter or deacon, let him and the person that ordained him be deprived; and let him be entirely cut off from communion, as Simon Magus was by me Peter" (*Constitutions of the Holy Apostles* 8.47.30 [ANF 7:501]).

39. Dudden, *Gregory the Great*, 46-48, 68-69.

40. Markus, *Gregory the Great*, 172-75. In one letter, Gregory comments specifically on the office of bishop, remarking, "We have learnt that their office is handled with such great presumption there that laymen are suddenly consecrated as bishops, and that is extremely serious. But what are those men going to do, what will they provide for their people, who aspire to being made bishops not to benefit the people, but for their own honor?" He goes on to label this as "simoniacal heresy" (Gregory the Great, *Letters*, 2:676-77).

41. Goez, "Simonie," 1329.

The heresy plagued the Church through the Middle Ages, even spreading its roots into monasticism[42] and eventually leading to the Investiture Controversy, which received official address in the Concordat of Worms in the twelfth-century.[43] By the thirteenth century, the heresy afflicted even the papal office, with Nicholas III serving as the prime example. For this reason, Dante encounters Nicholas in the eighth circle and third ditch of hell, "where the Simonists are set,"[44] who is awaiting the arrival of his successor, Boniface VIII, and is stuffed in a hole, upside down with his feet sticking in the air as an ironic reversal of his role as the head of the Church because he abused his position.

The name Simon Magus immediately brought simony to mind in the ninth century. Haimo's reference to Simon comes from and feeds into the ongoing repulsion toward simony. This provides the ecclesiastical context for Haimo's use of the name Simon Magus. The apocryphal nature of his reference derives from another source.

The allusion to Simon deceiving an executioner by substituting a ram comes from the fourth-century work *The Acts of Peter and Paul*. In this text, Peter, Paul, and Simon find themselves in the presence of Nero, who has pronounced Simon to be a god. Following a number of pseudo-magical feats and claiming messianic titles for himself, Simon flies through the air at a great height only to plummet to his death after Peter prays that the demons holding Simon aloft release him. Nero, who believed Simon to be divine, responds by having Peter and Paul executed.

Of note in this story are not only the false signs that Simon performs and which the apostles reveal to be false, but also Simon's claim to be the

---

42. This manifested particularly in the Benedictine (Haimo's order) monasteries of France, in that monastic candidate were expected to pay for their entry into the order. See Lynch, *Simoniacal Entry*, esp. 83–106.

43. Lindberg, *Brief History of Christianity*, 66–68. Alongside clerical marriage, simony was the major catalyst for the papal reforms of the eleventh and twelfth centuries. See Thomson, *Western Church*, 82–85.

44. Dante Alighieri, *Inferno*, Canto XIX. This brief history on Simony is not intended to neglect the Reformation discussion of simony, but rather to give a writing context for Haimo. Indeed, Luther spoke frequently on the topic of simony and changed the trajectory of the discourse. He argued that the papacy, bishops, and the like were not guilty of simony when it came to selling offices or accepting payment for the pallium. This crime was bribery, not simony. True simony, in Luther's vision, is impossible, because it entails the sale of gifts of the Holy Spirit, which no one can accomplish. Those who claim to sell remission of sins or other graces of God, which are spiritual goods, do so falsely. Therefore, Luther restricts the broader definition of simony adopted by Haimo and other medieval theologians. See Luther, *Lectures on Genesis 21–25* (LW 4:109–205).

Son of God, his receiving circumcision, his "resurrection" after three days, his claim that he will ascend to heaven, and the use and application of the very words of Christ to himself.[45] Simon Magus is set up as the reverse replica of Christ such that he typifies the expected Antichrist.

Outside of the NT, Justin Martyr (d. 165) makes the earliest reference to Simon Magus, offering background information, describing his "miracles" as false, and revealing his claims to divinity.[46] Irenaeus follows his predecessor in his description of Simon, but adds to this that Simon is the source of a variety of heresies.[47] In these sources, Simon exhibits characteristics of the "Antichrist" in 2 Thessalonians.

In sources contemporary to *The Acts of Peter and Paul*, such as Cyril of Jerusalem's *Catechetical Lectures* and a Pseudo-Hippolytan homily, the conflation of Simon Magus with Antichrist is in full effect.[48] Cyril describes the Antichrist as a highly skilled magician,[49] while Pseudo-Hippolytus comments on the Antichrist's ability to fly by means of demonic levitation.[50] Thus Haimo accesses a developed tradition of the text history of Acts 8:9–24 and 2 Thess 2.

Considering these ecclesial and apocryphal sources materials, Haimo's decision to include Simon Magus in this particular section of 2 Thessalonians is striking, because he has drawn together two significant strands of thought regarding Simon.[51] Not only is simony implicitly condemned,

---

45. *Acts of the Holy Apostles* (ANF 8:477–85). Reference to this apocryphal work appears again in twelfth-century Reims with regard to witchcraft during an event in which a woman a woman flew out of a window, carried "by the ministry of evil spirits who once caught Simon Magus up into the air" (Wakefield and Evans, *Heresies*, 253).

46. Justin's language bears a striking resemblance to Thess 2:3–4, 9, 11. See Justin Martyr, *Apologia* 1.26 (PG 6:26).

47. Irenaeus, *Adversus Haeresies* 1.23.2 (PG 7:671–72).

48. McGinn, *Antichrist*, 70–71, 74; Bousset, *Antichrist Legend*, 146–47. This conflation likely follows from Origen, who identified Simon as Antichrist in an immanent sense. See Origen, *Commentaria in Evangelium* (PG 13:1643, 1659); McGinn, *Antichrist*, 300n64.

49. Cyril of Jerusalem, *Catacheses* 15:11 (PG 33:884).

50. Pseudo-Hippolytus, *De consummatione mundi* 29 (PG 10:933).

51. Predestination and Simon Magus are brought together in a thirteenth-century work that describes a heretical group that holds to the position that God predestines all good things, while the devil preordains all evil things—a position attributed by their accusers to Simon Magus. Wakefield and Evans, *Heresies*, 275. In the "Life of Gregory VII (1128)," Paul of Bernried reports the accusation that Henry IV was guilty of simony and described him as the "precursor of the Antichrist," yet this applies primarily to Henry's attempt to undermine the papacy and establish his own pope. See Paul of Bernried, "Life

but Haimo also identifies any cleric who pays for their position with the Antichrist.

The contention could be taken even further to claim that Haimo perceives these clergy as the "mystery of iniquity" already at work (2:7) in the line of Nero, Diocletian, and Julian the Apostate.[52] His commentary on Ezekiel strengthens this argument, for in it he openly describes bishops and priests who pay for their positions as lions and wolves, who consume their poor congregants and drag them into hell by their unauthorised and false administration of their office.[53] If these men prefigure Antichrist, then any miracles that occur under their administration, such as the transubstantiation[54] of the Eucharist, the crux of the Carolingian orthodox faith, does not genuinely occur. We see precisely such a concern arise over the effects of simony and lay investiture on the Eucharist in the eleventh and twelfth centuries.[55]

Therefore, Haimo's interpretation of 2 Thessalonians with reference to Simon Magus is not merely provocative to his horizon of expectations. The monk has levelled a polemical challenge to the ecclesial realm by access to an interpretive tradition.

In one sense Haimo models his work after Fathers like Irenaeus, Tertullian, and Augustine,[56] who wrote extensively against heresies. Despite converging contexts that nurture exegetical attention to heresy, Haimo remains unique for his time period in his inclusion of Simon in his commentary on 2 Thessalonians—this marks the way in which he surpasses his horizon of expectations.

Because of this distinctiveness, Lombard's reference to the heretic at exactly the same location (2:9) in his commentary on the epistle renders

---

of Gregory VII," 310–14.

52. Haimo of Auxerre, *In epist. ii ad Thess* (PL 117:781).

53. We might also add to this his commentaries on Romans, Galatians, and Ephesians. See Contreni, "By Lions," esp. 38–43.

54. Admittedly, the term "transubstantiation" is anachronistic, but a belief in the real presence and "metamorphosis" of the elements antedates Haimo. For example: "τοῦτό ἐστιν τὸ σῶμά μου, φησί. Τοῦτο τὸ ῥῆμα μεταρρυθμίζει τὰ προκείμενα" (John Chrysostom, *De proditione Judae* 1.6 [PG 49:380] [emphasis added]).

55. Pelikan, *Christian Tradition*, 3:212–13; Colish, *Peter Lombard*, 2:575–80.

56. In Augustine, *Heresies* 1; *Answer to an Enemy of the Law and the Prophets* 2.12.40, Augustine regards Simon as the inaugural heretic, in keeping with several other Fathers (e.g., Eusebius) and following on from Irenaeus. See Augustine, *Arianism and Other Heresies*, 1.18:34, 440, respectively.

it conspicuous. He even makes use of the same example in which Simon substitutes a ram for himself at his execution. Lombard points primarily to Simon's claim of divinity as evidence that his miraculous signs are lies. Even should they legitimately produce a genuine effect, it is only performed by the *permission* of God in order to attract the perishing to the larger mendacity.[57] Haimo, despite Lombard's rewording of his predecessor on 2 Thessalonians, exerts commanding influence over the latter.[58] By Lombard's day, however, Haimo's reading has lost its causticness and already requires reading against the grain to restore its tone.

Apocalyptic Realism

Though the arguably more interesting apocalyptic material appears in 2 Thess 2, Haimo briefly introduces this perspective in chapter 1. He notes that God permits all things to take place, including the suffering of the righteous in this life (1:4). Yet their suffering assures the reversal of their fate with the wicked in the Judgment (1:6), when the Lord afflicts the wicked (i.e., the pagans, heretics, false Christians, and the Jews) with the flame of fire (1:8). These will suffer eternal punishment (1:9), even if it should mean that they "give" punishment to one another, witnessing the coming of Christ as terrible and fierce. Ambrosiaster, Haimo's main patristic interlocutor, speaks of the "double meaning" of the Lord's second advent (1:10), in that "Christ will come to punish the bad and glorify the good," appearing "brilliant (*clarus*) and wonderful" to the former.[59] Similarly, Haimo summarizes the apocalyptic dualism of the Lord's appearance in his second advent as "brilliant (*clarus*) and enticing, but to the reprobate terrible and fierce."[60]

Hundreds of years later, Peter Lombard (d. 1160) picks up on this double meaning in his commentary on 2 Thessalonians, using Haimo, yet also clarifying that the meaning extends not just to the Lord's appearance, but also his action. His advent means punishment or glorification for the respective groups. Haimo does not deny this, but Lombard sees the necessity

---

57. Peter Lombard, *In epist. ii ad Thess* (PL 192:320–21). Later in this chapter, we discuss how Lombard uses Haimo and Ambrosiaster as a foil for the "correct" reading found in Augustine. This rule, however, does not apply to all of Lombard's use of Haimo on 2 Thessalonians.
58. Colish, *Peter Lombard*, 1:205–7.
59. Ambrosiaster, *Ad Thessalonicenses secunda* (CSEL 81:237).
60. Haimo of Auxerre, "Exposition," 23.

of clarifying the effect of Christ's appearance.[61] Again, the old mediates the new—despite the distillation, Ambrosiaster instigates the qualified readings of Haimo and Lombard, and an 800-year interpretive tradition. With these preliminary notes in mind, which show Haimo's apocalyptic reading persists throughout the letter, we can turn to the second chapter.

In the *argumentum*, Haimo ostensibly turns to Jerome for the explanation of Paul's nebulous description of the fall of the Roman Empire as due to the fear that open discussion of the topic would lead to unnecessary persecution of the Church.[62] At the same time, the absence of verbal overlap and the fact that several Fathers[63] held this view indicates that this was a common idea circulating during that period. Nevertheless, Jerome's *Epistle 121* seems to be the primary patristic source for Haimo's reading of 2 Thess 2:1–10, which comprises the bulk of his commentary and what he perceives as the paramount material that Paul wanted to communicate in writing the epistle.[64]

In point eleven of this letter to Algasia, Jerome summarizes Paul's reason for writing 2 Thessalonians in response to misunderstanding(s) of the first epistle. Regarding "the coming of our Lord Jesus Christ and of our gathering into him," the Church Father comments on the dual advents of Christ—the first in humility and the second in glory.[65] Haimo includes Jerome's view at the same verse, but compresses it slightly. He also describes

---

61. "Ipse enim clarus et mirabilis videbitur in credentibus; severus autem apparebit in incredulous, cum eos poenis aeternis coarctabit. Et est horum verborum brevis sensus. Veniet punier malos, et glorificare bonos, quia creditum" (Lombard, *In epistolam ii ad Thessalonicenses* [PL 192:315]).

62. Jerome, *Epistle 121* (CSEL 56.3.54). In the notes on his translation of Haimo's text, Hughes cites Jerome and Ambrosiaster as potential sources, but Ambrosiaster makes a slightly different point in his argumentum, adding that the letter outlines the "tribulation of some of the brothers." See Ambrosiaster, *Ad Thessalnicenses secunda* (CSEL 81.3.235); Haimo of Auxerre, "Exposition," 32.

63. Cf. John Chrysostom, *In epist. ii ad Thess* 4 (FCT 5:472–73).

64. It is significant to note that, following 2:10, the final verse upon which Jerome comments, Haimo returns to using Ambrosiaster. At 2:14, for example, Haimo describes the acquisition of Lord's glory as believers working "for the increase of the body of Christ" (augmentum faciatis corpori Christi) (Haimo of Auxerre, *In epist. ii ad Thess* [PL 117:782]); cf. "adquiruntur ad *augmentum* gloriae *corporis Christi*" and "quique enim deserto Diablo . . . *augmentum faciunt* deo in *corpore Christi*" (both on 2:14) (Ambrosiaster, *Ad Thess sec.* [CSEL 81:242] [emphasis added]).

65. "Duos autem esse aduentus domini saluatoris et omnia prophetarum docent uolumina et euangeliorum fides, quod primum in humilitate uenerit et postea sit uenturus in gloria" (Jerome, *Epistle 121* [CSEL 56.3.51–52]).

the Second-Coming of Christ, though in terms of "judgment" rather than "glory." It seems that this reading makes more sense of the letter's content than the uninvolved or generic term "glory." Jerome's question "What is the focus of the epistle?" and even his answer mediates Haimo's reading, which hears a different response to the question in light of predominant topics in chapters 1 and 2: the judgment of the wicked and Antichrist.

Shortly thereafter, Haimo quotes part of 2 Thess 2:2 and offers a concrete example of what it means not to "be frightened, as if the day of the Lord approaches . . . by a word." Haimo suggests, "If someone says to you that he is an exegete and interpreter of prophecies: 'I have gathered the meaning of the prophet Isaiah and Daniel and the other prophets, and I foresee that the Day of Judgment is imminent and that Christ is coming to judge.' . . . Do not be afraid."[66] Interestingly, this appears to be a loose paraphrase of what Jerome described as the potential situation that gave rise to Paul's necessity for writing the letter.[67] In Haimo's commentary, though, it functions as both a warning in the mouth of the apostle to the historical congregation and to the present reader of Haimo's work. This point feeds into our larger discussion of sermon preparation and apocalyptic toward the end of this chapter. It would suffice to add that Haimo might be attempting to quell any apocalyptic predictions following the coronation of Charlemagne and leading up to the year 1,000.[68] Jerome and Haimo both write for pastoral reasons, yet in Haimo's excitable context, he hears in Paul's own wording a response to the question, "What if someone predicts 'The end is nigh?'" Haimo expands Jerome's reading and provokes his own horizon of expectations.

Regarding whether Christ or his archangel Michael destroys Antichrist (2:8), Haimo comments that it is irrelevant, because his destruction will come about by Christ's power. This issue does not present itself from the text of 2 Thessalonians, but from the divergent views of the Fathers. Most Fathers, Jerome included,[69] hold that Christ will destroy Antichrist. Gregory, however, presents the conundrum that Haimo seeks to resolve

---

66. Haimo of Auxerre, "Exposition," 24–25.

67. cf. "Igitur Thessalonicensium animos . . . uel aliquorum coniectura Esaiae et Danihelis euangeliorum que uerba de antichristo praenuntiantia in illud tempus interpretantium mouerat atque turbauerat, ut in maiestate sua tunc Christum sperant esse uenturum" (Jerome, *Epistle 121* [CSEL 56.3.55]).

68. See Landes, "Fear of an Apocalyptic Year," esp. 110–45.

69. Jerome, *Epistle 121* (CSEL 56.3.54).

by seemingly asserting both positions in different works.[70] Because of the Fathers, a new problem has presented itself in the history of 2 Thessalonians. Haimo resolves the difficulty of the divergent readings by subsuming "Christ" and "Michael" under the answer "Christ's power." This change is not substantial, but it is a shift in the reception of 2 Thessalonians.

Haimo's reading of chapter 2 comprises approximately 60 percent of his commentary and is dominated by a literal reading in the tone of Jerome and Ambrosiaster. He begins with the introductory note that the "coming of our Lord Jesus Christ" (2:1) renders lucid the purpose of the chapter. Regarding the key phrases of the chapter, Haimo asserts that "the desertion" (*discessio*; 2:3) is the dissolution of the Roman Empire; the "man of sin" (2:3) is Antichrist; "the temple of God" (2:4) may refer to either the Jerusalem temple or the Church; the Roman Empire is "what restrains" (*detineat*; 2:6); the "mystery of iniquity" (2:7) is the work of the devil in persecuting and murdering the saints through "his members" (i.e., Nero, Diocletian, and Julian); the Roman emperor is "the one who restrains" (2:7) as the individual representative of the corporate power of Empire, who prefigures Antichrist.[71] There are several important points to his reading to draw out regarding the Millennium and the Antichrist.

The Sabbatical Millennium

Though it appears at times that Haimo sees the "rule of the Romans as not yet destroyed, nor have all the nations deserted them"[72] as his reality, closer attention reveals that, in these instances, he speaks as though from the *apostle's present*, clarifying his point to the Thessalonians. This makes sense of how Haimo can, at the same time, refer to the collapse of the Roman Empire, "which we already see fulfilled."[73] If this were not the case, Haimo would have no reason to account for the delay in Antichrist's

---

70. See Gregory the Great, *Homiliae in Evangelia* 34.9 (CCSL 141:307) for the former; *Moralia in Iob* 32.15.26-27 (CCSL 143B:1650) for the latter. The difficulty is, in fact, a bit more complex, as Gregory asserts that Michael will destroy *Satan* (though he remains unnamed) in homily 34 on the Gospels, and that Christ will destroy the *Antichrist* "non angelorum bello" in his *Moralia*.

71. Haimo of Auxerre, *In epist. ii ad Thess* (PL 117:779-81). On this argument, see Hughes, *Constructing Antichrist*, 155-58.

72. Haimo of Auxerre, "Exposition," 27.

73. "Quod jam nos impletum videmus" (Haimo of Auxerre, *In epist. ii ad Thess* [PL 117:780]).

arrival.⁷⁴ Given the apocalyptic climate of the ninth century and the history of exegesis with regard to the projected Day of the Lord, Haimo has made a unique move. One might expect at this point a discussion of the Church's present existence in the sabbatical millennium, which should precede the arrival of Antichrist.⁷⁵

The brilliance of his reading lies in the complete absence of a discussion regarding the sabbatical millennium and its relationship to the arrival of Antichrist. Even more, Haimo undermines the entire concept of the millennium and precise dating of apocalyptic events. The Christian expectation of a sabbatical millennium can be traced as early as the *Epistle of Barnabas* 7: "According to this theory, since the world was created in six days and God rested on the seventh, and since 'a thousand years is as a day in the sight of the Lord,' this fallen world of travail would last for six thousand years and then, finally, would come the sabbatical millennium."⁷⁶ In this line of thinking, the Church developed the *annus mundi* dating system in the third century to predict the coming (prolonged) Sabbath, which it anticipated would begin in 500 CE.⁷⁷ As this date approached, however,

---

74. "Tunc revelabitur ille iniquus postquam fuerit destructum Romanum imperium, non est ita intelligendum, quod statim dixerit illum venturum, sed primum illud destruendum, ac deinde Antichristum venturum, tempore a Deo disposito" (Haimo of Auxerre, *In epist. ii ad Thess* [PL 117:781]).

75. Haimo does precisely this in his Revelation commentary. The millennium must precede the Antichrist, but, for Haimo, 1,000 is simply an expression of perfection not to be taken literally. See Haimo of Auxerre, *Expos. in Apoc.* (PL 117:1182).

76. Landes, "Fear of an Apocalyptic Year," 110. For more detail on Barnabas as an early source for Christian millenarianism, see Landes, "Lest the Millennium Be Fulfilled," 141–44.

77. After *Barnabas*, early Christian sources for millennial expectations were the chronographies of Theophilus of Antioch and Clement of Alexandria. The most influential early authors in this regard, however, were Hippolytus and Lactantius. See Hippolytus of Rome, *On Daniel* 4 (*ANF* 5:179); Lactantius, *The Divine Institutes* 7.14 (*ANF* 7:211–12). For a detailed discussion on Hippolytus as the primary source for early millenarianism, see Landes, "Lest the Millennium Be Fulfilled," 144–49.

Receiving 2 Thessalonians

Christian scholars[78] revised their prediction to 800 CE, which, as it would turn out, was the year of Charlemagne's coronation.[79]

As the deadline approached again, Bede proposed a new dating system (*annus Domini*) with the incarnation functioning as its basis. The millennium received a new lease on life, but Bede also hoped to silence the questions of "rustics" regarding the impending arrival of the millennium (i.e., 800). Though Bede sought by his work and the *annus Domini* system to completely undermine any millenarianism,[80] this left the years between 800 and 1000/1033 in a state of suspended, eschatological expectation, punctuated with occasional and regionally limited chiliastic outbreaks.[81] Thietland of Einsiedeln (d. 965) reflects such expectation in his commentary on 2 Thessalonians when he reads the *revelation* of "the lawless one" (2:8) as identical with the *release* of the dragon, who was bound in Christ's passion, after 1,000 years of imprisonment (Rev 20:1–3).[82]

The complete absence of the millennium from Haimo's commentary, therefore, renders his discussion as contextually conspicuous. In one sense, he observes Augustine's caution toward millennial expectations, yet different from the Church Father, Haimo does not appear to endorse any dating system (*annus mundi* or *annus Domini*) that would allow one to project the beginning of a new millennium. If anything, according to chiliastic expectations, Antichrist should have arrived generations ago after the fall of Rome. Thus, Haimo completely undercuts the ability to reliably propose the date of the Day of the Lord. His reading allows for either the *annus*

78. This began with Eusebius, whose view Jerome, Augustine, and Orosius endorsed. None of the above supported the idea of a sabbatical millennium, but the chronology that they embraced, nevertheless, placed the year 6,000 AM in 800 CE. For Eusebius's summary of his own calculations, see Burgess's translation of Eusebius's *Chronici canones* (Burgess, *Studies*, 65). For Eusebius's reaction to Hippolytus, see Landes, "Lest the Millennium Be Fulfilled," 149–56.

79. The coronation took place on December 25, 800—the first day of the new millennium. Brandes and Landes observe that the confluence of this date and the coronation would not have gone unnoticed. See Brandes, "Anastasios ὁ Δίκρος," 27; Landes, "Fear of an Apocalyptic Year," 114–15. Hughes adds to the discussion that Leo III may have been invoking the pseudo-Methodian "last world emperor" myth in coronating Charlemagne on this date, with the expectation of inaugurating the "millennium of peace" (Hughes, *Constructing Antichrist*, 127).

80. cf. Bede the Venerable, *De temporum ratione* 67 (CCSL 123B:535–37).

81. Landes, "Fear of an Apocalyptic Year," 113–16.

82. Thietland of Einselden, "In epist. ii ad Thess," 55–56. Cartwright observes that Thietland's preference for "release" over "revelation" allows him to incorporate the discussion on Rev 20 (Cartwright, "Thietland's Commentary on 2 Thessalonians," 98).

mundi or *annus Domini* dating systems, but he subverts their power in the hands of the chiliast. In this regard, Haimo characterizes a tendency that crystallizes in Carolingian-Bedan theology: avoidance of universal history and denunciation of the sabbatical millennium.[83] The former is clear in his commentary; the latter is implicit.

This approach to the millennium coheres with Haimo's broader Augustinian-agnosticism toward the chronology of eschatological events in 2 Thess 2. Nevertheless, this does not hamper Haimo's confidence in asserting the events that must take place and their sequence, according to 2 Thessalonians. His apocalyptic timeline looks like this:

> *discessio* from Rome→ (*unknown length of time*)→ the advent of Antichrist→ (*unknown length of time*)→ Christ/Michael destroys Antichrist→ (*unknown length of time*)→ the Final Judgment.

Furthermore, his commentary on Revelation (in which he describes all time following the redemption of the cross as eschatological) appears to nurture this uncertainty and align him even more closely with Augustine.[84] That is to say, predictions about the "millennium" or even the "end" overlook the fact that the eschatological age has already begun. Different from Augustine, though, Haimo's interpretation of 2 Thessalonians is *entirely literal* and punctuated with temporal uncertainties.[85] Only through restoring Haimo's horizon of expectations does *Rezeptionsästhetik* disclose the aesthetic high point and provocative nature of his reading.

As already noted, Haimo diverges from Bede (who simply quotes Augustine) and Thietland (who harmonizes 2 Thessalonians and Revelation for an eschatological timeline). His reading largely resonates with Rabanus and Sedulius, who, though they largely quote Theodore and Pelagius, respectively, quote them in such a way as to advance a historical-literal reading of 2 Thessalonians. That it is to say, the three generally agree that 2 Thessalonians should be read as a literal account of events to come. Rabanus and Sedulius likewise offer no discussion of the millennium, but that can be attributed to their copying the Fathers.

They diverge from one another, however, in Rabanus's and Sedulius's inclusion of the Latin spiritual interpretation at certain crucial junctures

---

83. Landes, "Lest the Millennium Be Fulfilled," 180–81.

84. Lobrichon, "Stalking the Signs," 73–74.

85. Also, Haimo clearly sees the fall of Rome as coming after Paul, likely in the reign of Constantine, while Augustine argues that the power of the Empire collapsed in the cross.

in their commentaries. Rabanus, for example, quotes Augustine's reading of "what now restrains" (2 Thess 2:6) as the wicked and false individuals within the Church who must reach a critical-mass for Antichrist before he bursts on to the scene.[86]

Similarly, Sedulius perceives the "mystery of iniquity" (2:7) is both the foreshadowing of and "the presence of the Antichrist himself"[87] in those who teach false doctrine. He also clearly believes that the Roman Empire has not fallen, and that Antichrist will only arrive after the appearance of another "restraining force," that is, another Nero.[88]

Haimo, therefore, is strikingly unique in his capacity to embrace, yet hold separate his genre-attentive approaches to 2 Thessalonians and Revelation. For Haimo, "the Latin spiritual interpretation and the literal apocalyptic realism are valid interpretations of the apocalyptic tradition, but they should not be confused."[89] Thus one can call Haimo an apocalyptic realist, but not exclusively.

Generations later, Peter Lombard takes up Haimo's reading of 2 Thess 2 in a pejorative manner. Though it appears he offers a catena of Haimo, Ambrosiaster, and Augustine, the organisation of the materials, in fact, reveals his castigation of the former two with the latter. For example, he introduces the view held by Haimo and Ambrosiaster that the "mystery of iniquity at work" (2:7) is a way for the apostle to refer obliquely to Nero, then he follows this with Augustine's scathing reprimand of all individuals who have read the "restraining force" (2:6) as Rome and Nero as the "mystery of iniquity" (2:7). The placement of the material gives Augustine the last, corrective word and denigrates the apocalyptic realist reading of 2 Thessalonians.[90] Haimo functions as a foil for Lombard against which to read Augustine, at least in regards to portions of 2 Thess 2:1–12. Augustine's perspective becomes a more comfortable reading in the generations further from the fall of Rome and thereby becomes a voice of dominance. Yet Haimo's reading better addresses the apparently conflicting eschatologies of the NT and the question of the millennium that arises from a canonical reading of scripture.

---

86. Rabanus Maurus, *Exposito in epist. ii ad Thess* (PL 116:572).

87. Hughes, *Constructing Antichrist*, 143.

88. Hughes, *Constructing Antichrist*, 143–44; Sedulius Scotus, *In epist. ii ad Thess* (PL 103:223).

89. Hughes, *Constructing Antichrist*, 165.

90. Peter Lombard, *In epist. ii ad Thess* (PL 192:318–19).

Elsewhere in Haimo's corpus we see the same sensitivity to contemporary anxiety regarding the millennium. In a sermon on the Second Sunday of Advent, Haimo offers a sermon that begins with Luke 21:25. Much like Jesus with his disciples, Haimo attempts to assuage the concerns of his audience by describing the events of the *eschaton* so that they may be prepared when it arrives. He articulates the arrival of the Antichrist, noting that he will oppose and exalt himself above "all that is called God or that is worshipped" (2 Thess 2:4).[91] Particularly in an age of erratic apocalyptic upheaval, Haimo's comments on 2 Thess 2 appropriately guide a reader into a balanced and cautious reading of the epistle.

Haimo's Antichrist

Turning to a more concentrated dimension of Haimo's reading of 2 Thess 2:1–12, we briefly attend to his picture of Antichrist. Following Thiselton, we recognize several perspectives on Antichrist in the early Church that can be distilled into six basic approaches for understanding this entity: Antichrist is (1) the devil; (2) an individual, though a tool of Satan; (3) a man *and* a corporate figure; (4) a "reverse replica" of Christ; (5) a magician, and; (6) "a principle, applicable to the present and to all times."[92] By the ninth century, Haimo had a diverse and developed view of Antichrist from which to draw for his commentary, and he describes the title "man of sin" (2:3) for Antichrist as appropriate, because he will be a man and "the source of all sins." He clarifies this later in asserting that Antichrist will lead people to worship the devil by means of "lying signs and wonders" (2:9).

In a somewhat Hippolytan manner, he argues that the title "son of damnation" (2:3) means "son of the devil," though he qualifies that this is only by imitation and not by nature. In these two ways (i.e., performing false miracles and sonship via imitation) Antichrist is an *imperfect* reverse replica of Christ. In a similar manner, he points out that Antichrist "displaying himself *as if he were* a god" (2:4), reflects how "just as the fullness of divinity reposed in Christ, so the fullness of vice and every iniquity will dwell in that person called Antichrist."[93]

---

91. Haimo of Auxerre, *Homiliae de Tempore* 2 (PL 117:19).

92. These perspectives were not seen as mutually exclusive. See Thiselton, *1 and 2 Thessalonians*, 217 (for the full discussion, see 213–17).

93. Haimo of Auxerre, "Exposition," 26.

He adds to this point that the devil will possess him, "but he will not give up his senses," thereby remaining culpable for his iniquity.[94] It is crucial to Haimo that one recognize Antichrist's limited function within the sovereignty of God, particularly in the time of his manifestation and his ability to deceive those who are perishing.[95]

One final point regarding Antichrist secures Haimo's apocalyptic realist reading of 2 Thessalonians over against Augustine. He recognizes "the mystery of iniquity at work" (2:7) in the persecuting emperors of the Roman Empire as "members" of Antichrist, but only in the sense that they prefigure his arrival. As Hughes correctly notes, Haimo does not make use of the "corporal metaphor,"[96] but this likely stems from his view of the parallels between Christ and Antichrist. Operating within this framework, it would be difficult for Haimo to suggest that a body of individuals were "Christ" before the incarnation. Alternatively several characters of the OT (e.g., Abel, Isaac, and David) *prefigure* Christ.[97]

Several generations prior to Haimo, Isidore of Seville (d. 636) exerted considerable influence on medieval theologians through his *Etymologia*, and Haimo makes frequent use of the work elsewhere,[98] so its absence from the 2 Thessalonians commentary is noteworthy, though understandable. When writing about Satan, Isidore notes that this title means "adversary" or "transgressor," and that elsewhere he is called "Antichrist (*Antichristus*), because he is to come against Christ."[99] Isidore's primary interest is the desire to clarify that this means "against Christ" rather than "before (*ante*) Christ," as some appear to have argued.

This reading, however, misses the very distinction held in 2 Thess 2:9 that "the coming of the lawless one is by the activity of Satan." Additionally, this perspective jeopardizes a crucial element of Haimo's understanding that Antichrist is the reverse replica of Christ (i.e., Christ comes from

---

94. Haimo of Auxerre, "Exposition," 26, 29. We witness precisely such an intimate relationship between Antichrist and the devil in the famous sixteenth-century painting by Luca Signorelli, *Deeds of the Antichrist*, in which it is difficult to tell where Antichrist ends and Satan, whispering into his ear, begins.

95. "Ac deinde Antichristum venturum, tempore a Deo disposito" and "[Deus] permittet ad eos venire Antichristum operatorem mendacii" (Haimo of Auxerre, *In epist. ii ad Thess* [PL 117:781, 782, respectively]).

96. Hughes, *Constructing Antichrist*, 158.

97. Haimo of Auxerre, *In epist. ii ad Thess* (PL 117:781).

98. Boucaud, "Claude de Turin," 110; Heil, "Theodulf," 117–18.

99. Isidore of Seville, *Etymologies*, 8.11.19–20.

the Father and Antichrist comes from the devil). Fortunately, Haimo can take refuge in the orthodox readings of Jerome and Ambrosiaster, while Isidore's interpretation finds its roots in Pelagius.[100] Haimo's work sees that a particular tradition survives and silences a maverick reading that had influential potential. We realize this in the fact that both Thomas Aquinas and Bonaventure cite Haimo favourably for this interpretation, though qualifying that humanity is not taken into the person of the devil in the same way that it was into God the Son. Instead, the devil has a greater level of influence over the Antichrist than other people.[101]

Given Isidore's view above, it is interesting that Sedulius proceeds with a different reading of Antichrist. When introducing the "man of sin" (2:3), Pelagius's commentary reads "*Et revelatus fuerit homo peccati. Diaboli scilicet.*"[102] Sedulius clarifies Pelagius's reading thus: "*Homo. Antichristus. Peccati. Diaboli scilicet*"[103] thereby remaining close to Haimo: Antichrist is *of* the devil (the subjective genetive). Yet in suggesting that the "mystery of iniquity" (2:7) is a corporate Antichrist body preceding the arrival of an individual Antichrist, Sedulius fuses the spiritual reading of Augustine with literal reading of Pelagius. Haimo holds these perspectives apart on literary grounds, and sees "the mystery of iniquity at work" as Antichrist working through his members (without labelling them "Antichrist") in the present through the dissemination of false doctrines. In the same way that Christ works through his members presently to proclaim the truth, so too Antichrist spreads "the lie" in a reflective way, such as simony—a suggestive assault on the Church in Haimo's day.[104]

---

100. Though Isidore misreads Pelagius at this point, Pelagius is the historical root of this tradition nonetheless. Pelagius's commentary reads "*Et revelatus fuerit homo peccati. Diaboli scilicet.*" If *diaboli* is taken as nominative, then it would mean the devil *is* Antichrist. If, however, one reads it as a genitive (with the case of *peccati*, which is more likely), it is describing the "revelation of the man of sin, namely [the man] of the devil," thus equating "sin" with "devil." This becomes clearer in the line that follows, in which Pelagius describes the devil possessing Antichrist, "as if he was born to him" (Pelagius, "Exposito in ii Thess," 443; cf. Bornemann, *Die Thessalonicherbriefe*, 403-4; Thiselton, *1 and 2 Thessalonians*, 216; Hughes, *Constructing Antichrist*, 69–70).

101. Thomas Aquinas, *ST* 3.8.8; Bonaventure, *Opera Omnia*, 8.232-33.

102. "*And the revealing of the man of sin.* Namely, *of the Devil*" (Pelagius, "Exposito in ii Thess," 443).

103. "*Man. Antichrist. Of Sin. Namely, of the Devil*" (Sedulius Scotus, *In epist. ii ad Thess* [PL 103:223]). I follow Sedulius's reading of *diaboli* as a genitive singular against Thiselton, who reads this as a nominative singular. Thiselton, *1 and 2 Thessalonians*, 222.

104. Thiselton, *1 and 2 Thessalonians*, 222.

In spirit with Haimo, Rabanus proposes that the providence of God "restrains" Antichrist. This would summarise Haimo's broader perspective, despite the fact that he sees the "restrainer" (2:7) as the Roman emperor and "that which restrains" (2:6) as the Roman Empire. Because Rabanus selectively copies patristic texts, he has an overlap regarding what restrains Antichrist: God's providence and the number of members that compose Antichrist's body. If one sees the former as governing the latter, however, the issue is easily resolved. Furthermore, for Rabanus, the "lying works" (2:9) are primarily doctrinal or theological, and anyone who "denies that Christ is God is an Antichrist."[105] Lastly, in keeping with Augustine and Gregory, Rabanus views the "mystery of iniquity" (2:7) as members of Antichrist's body who must reach a certain mass before Antichrist is revealed. Again, Haimo stands out as an abnormality for his refusal to incorporate the Latin spiritual tradition.

As noted above, Haimo relies more heavily on the Latin tradition of Jerome for his reading of 2 Thessalonians 2:1–10, and the only point at which Haimo opts for a reading from Jerome not found in *Epistle 121* is when he takes up his commentary on Daniel in order to name the location of Antichrist's death: the Mount of Olives.[106] The Lord, or Michael by the Lord's power, will destroy Antichrist (2:8) "on his throne on the Mount Olivet in Babylon."[107] By locating his death at the place of Christ's ascension, Haimo carries forward this *tradition* of Antichrist operating as a reverse-replica of Christ that began with Hippolytus and Tertullian, and which most Fathers carried forward.[108] Haimo contributes to the reception history of 2 Thessalonians by reading the destruction of Antichrist according to Jerome's Daniel commentary.

The final example of Haimo's employment of Jerome appears at the same verse with which he concludes his letter. Noting that Antichrist comes with "every seduction of iniquity for those who are perishing" (2:10), Haimo observes that this refers to the Jews and Pagans "because they did not welcome the love of truth that they might be saved, that is . . . the Holy Spirit through whom the love of God is poured forth (*infunditur*) deep into

---

105. Rabanus Maurus, *Exposito in epist. ii ad Thess* (PL 116:572). English text from Hughes, *Constructing Antichrist*, 134.

106. Jerome, *Commentariorum in Danielem* (CCSL 75A:933–34); Hughes, *Constructing Antichrist*, 78–79.

107. Haimo of Auxerre, "Exposition," 28.

108. Thiselton, *1 and 2 Thessalonians*, 214–17.

our hearts."[109] This quote simultaneously summarizes and expands Jerome, who says, "[Antichrist deceives] by the permission of God on account of the Jews, who did not want to receive the love of truth, that is Christ, because the love of God is poured forth in (*diffusa est in*) the hearts of those who believe."[110]

Jerome's reading comes in response to the question he raises about why Antichrist is able to deceive people, even the elect, if that were possible (cf. 2 Thess 2:10; Matt 24:24). He answers this question with the statement above: God *allows* Antichrist to bring about the full condemnation of the Jews, who have not the love of God in their hearts.

Haimo's incorporation of Jerome on this point is significant and modified. First of all, he includes Pagans as condemned with the Jews, in keeping with his reading of 2 Thess 1:8 and Ambrosiaster's position.[111] Second, though he follows the point that God permits Antichrist to come and deceive the Pagans and Jews,[112] he remains unclear as to whether this brings about the complete condemnation of *all* Jews. In fact, in his commentary on Isaiah, Haimo asserts that a number of Jews must convert to faith in Christ and will better resist Antichrist than Gentile converts.[113] Jerome carefully avoids discussing any final conversion of the Jews.[114] By paraphrasing Jerome, Haimo is able to incorporate the Father seamlessly into his work, appeal to his authority, and yet has to address a new question generated by the conflict between Jerome and his own reading of Isaiah.

In response to Antichrist setting himself up in the "temple of God, displaying himself as if he were a god" (2:4), Haimo proposes two patristic readings without attempting to resolve their differences. In the first example, he follows Hippolytus in suggesting that Antichrist will come from

---

109. Haimo of Auxerre, "Exposition," 29. Haimo of Auxerre, *In epist. ii ad Thess* (PL 117:782).

110. Jerome, *Epistle 121* (CSEL 56.3.55).

111. "Cum coeperit . . . ad dandum vindictum in paganos . . . et in Iudaeos" (Ambrosiaster, *Ad Thess sec.* [CSEL 81:237]; cf. Haimo of Auxerre, *In epist. i ad Thess* [PL 117:767]).

112. Haimo of Auxerre, "Exposition," 30.

113. Haimo of Auxerre, *Commentariorum in Isaiam* (PL 116:823-24, 880). It is important to note that Haimo also denied that the (unconverted) Jews would ever be redeemed—a perspective also against many of the Fathers. See Heil, "Labourers in the Lord's Quarry," 78.

114. Mégier, "Jewish Converts," 13-14.

Babylon and the tribe of Dan, that the Jews[115] will regard him as their Messiah, and that he will rebuild the temple in Jerusalem where he will receive worship.[116] In the second solution, Haimo points out that "the temple of God" could refer to the Church. Augustine and Jerome both make note of these two options for the meaning of "temple" and contend that the solution is uncertain.[117] Given his reliance on Jerome thus far, it seems likely that he draws the contention from here, though he does not confidently assert that "the Church" is a more probable interpretation as Jerome does.[118] Lastly, Chrysostom argues that it refers to both, in the sense that the worship of the Antichrist will extend out from the temple in Jerusalem into "every church."[119] Because his sources of authority are marked by an inconsistency, Haimo simply collects the options together and puts them in a contextual dialogue. Placing texts side-by-side, though helpful in illuminating a difficulty, amounts largely to imitation and a low register of aesthetic value. Nevertheless, Haimo concretizes the historic questions by posing them afresh in his horizon and reveals the importance of this tradition of questions.

CONCLUSION

He considers Paul's purpose in combating heresy and false doctrine as the guiding theme in his reading, and he articulates how this plays out at various moments in the letter and in his medieval context. In terms of originality and dissemination, Haimo is the most influential commentator on 2 Thessalonians from the Carolingian era, which we see evidenced in the way that his interpretation features alongside the Fathers in various *Glossae*, and that later scholastics rely on him for their own exegesis.

---

115. With the above noted exception. Bonaventure likewise cites this belief, but then notes the difficulty of this reading because it does not agree with Revelation, but then enlists Genesis 49:17 as the evidence in favor of the Danite Antichrist. Again, Haimo sets Revelation to one side, but he also alludes to the Genesis text. See Bonaventure, *Opera Omnia*, 100.

116. Hippolytus, *Christ and Antichrist* 6, 14–15 (ANF 5:206–7).

117. Augustine, *De civitate Dei* 20.19 (CCSL 48:731); Jerome *Epistle 121* (CSEL 56.3.53).

118. "Uel Hierosolymis, ut quidam putant, uel in ecclesia, ut uerius arbitramur" (Jerome *Epistle 121* [CSEL 56.3.53]).

119. John Chrysostom, *In epist. ii ad Thess* 4 (FCT 5:472–73).

As we have seen, one of the primary impulses in his interpretation of the epistle is the collective voice of the Church Fathers on 2 Thessalonians. Surprisingly unique from the Alcuinian camp, Haimo does not perceive the aim of preserving patristic thought as slavish regurgitation of their material. Instead, he extracts from their complex perspectives the kernel of their interpretation and interweaves it with his own thought in an easy to grasp manner. Haimo makes use of assertions by Jerome and Ambrosiaster regarding the restraining force as the Roman Empire to completely undercut any millenarian perspectives in his own time as a "mediation of the new through the old!"[120] Furthermore, the Carolingian monk exhibits a bold freedom from the booming voice of Augustine in the Middle Ages by considering first Paul's purpose in writing 2 Thessalonians and then pursuing his own reading.

Furthermore, Haimo carefully tows the line of single-predestination against the backdrop of the predestination controversy. Knowing that the Church condemned double-predestination as heresy, Haimo strikes a careful balance between the election of the faithful and the permissive will of God to allow the wicked to perish in keeping with their refusal "to welcome the love of the truth that they may be saved."[121] He introduces into the reception history of 2 Thessalonians the question of the permissive and predestining dimensions of God's sovereignty.

Haimo's relating Simon Magus to Antichrist bears several ramifications over simony and investiture in the medieval Church. In the reception history of this figure, Simon has developed from an obscure character in Acts 8:9–23, to being the first heretic of the Church, to a powerful, demonically-assisted opponent of Paul who prefigures Antichrist, to being conflated with Antichrist. In Haimo's work, these concepts converge and, placed in the context of 2 Thess 2:9, culminate in an implicit and sharp condemnation of clerics who receive their position by means of simony.

Finally, we see in Haimo caution regarding the *eschaton* and the events to precede it as shaped by the agnosticism of the biblical authors and Augustine on this topic, as well as the occasional chiliastic fervour of his age. Nevertheless, Paul's literal description of events to come provides Haimo the comfort of articulating an apocalyptic timeline within the confines of orthodoxy. By reading 2 Thessalonians in this manner, Haimo falls within the apocalyptic realist camp, but only in regard to this letter. He recognizes

---

120. Jauss, "Tradition," 375.
121. Haimo of Auxerre, "Exposition," 29.

the spiritual reading of Revelation as valid given the generic differences between the works. Within his apocalyptic realist approach to 2 Thessalonians, Haimo sees Antichrist as a literal figure, possessed by the devil, who, as the source of sin, will lead many to "believe in the lie" (2:12). He both perpetuates a tradition of interpretation and introduces a new element by rejecting the relationship of the epistle to the concept of the sabbatical millennium. Turning to our next interpreter, we find ourselves initially in the same region, though seven centuries later and in a time of great societal upheaval.

4

The Reformation
John Calvin

BACKGROUND

JOHN CALVIN WAS BORN into a *bourgeois* family in Noyon, France in 1509. Through his studies at the Universities of Paris (1520), Orléans (1527) and Bourges (1529),[1] Calvin came decidedly under the influence of Renaissance humanism, which emphasized studying classical texts apart from the mediation of commentaries or glosses, rigorous training in grammar and rhetoric,[2] and education in classical languages (occasionally including Hebrew). The first of these emphases materialised for Calvin through immediate study of the *Corpus iuris civilis* from the sixth century, which shaped the contours of civil law in Calvin's day.[3] By his university years, the Reformation(s) in Saxony and Zürich had gained significant momentum and was transitioning from localised annoyance to a legitimate threat to the Roman Church.

---

1. The dates from this point onward follow Parker's chronology. See Parker, *John Calvin*, 156–61.

2. "By the first half of the fifteenth century, the *studia humanitatis* came to stand for a clearly defined cycle of scholarly disciplines, namely grammar, rhetoric, history, poetry, and moral philosophy" (Kristeller, *Renaissance Thought*, 22).

3. Parker, *John Calvin*, 15.

Because of his associations with Protestantism, Calvin eventually sought asylum in Basel in 1535, where he published his first edition of the *Institutes* (1536)—a text that would function as a theological foundation for grappling with the remainder of his works. Within the year, he moved with Guillaume Farel to Geneva until their eviction over a theological dispute with the city Council in 1538, only to be summoned back to Geneva in 1541, where Calvin carried out his pastoral, scholarly, and civic duties until his death in 1564. By his life's conclusion he had published commentaries on most books of the Bible, numerous theological tractates, and he offered a final revision of the *Institutes* in 1559.[4]

Diachrony and The Synchronic Canon

As we discuss below, Augustine and Chrysostom exert a commanding influence on Calvin, but additional material from the Middle Ages following Haimo is important for aesthetic and diachronic considerations, including works from Berengar of Tours and Thomas á Kempis. In terms of the synchronic canon and Calvin's epochal moment, he wrote in the midst of a prolific community that attended especially to the contested meaning of 2 Thessalonians, most notably Luther, Melanchthon, and Zwingli from the Protestant camp, and Cajetan, Erasmus, and Estius from Catholicism.

2 Thessalonians Commentary and The Institutes: Provenance, Audience, and Structure

The sheer volume of Calvin's work virtually ensured that he would engage with 2 Thessalonians on a number of occasions. As the dedication to Benedict Textor in his commentary on the epistle indicates, Calvin authored this work in Geneva in 1550, and, as noted above, the final version of the *Institutes* in 1559. Other and infrequently utilized materials receive attention as they arise in our discussion.

In terms of the audience of these materials, Calvin published works first in Latin, to reach the broadest (including academics and clergy) audience, and then in the vernacular, French, for the readers native to his

---

4. Most of this background relies on Cottret, *Calvin*; Parker, *John Calvin*.

congregation. Needless to say, Calvin had a broad base of readership, from the average layperson to world leaders.[5]

When looking at the two primary sources for this reception history, the *Institutes* and the 2 Thessalonians commentary, their overall difference is best exemplified by the two primary patristic influences on Calvin's work: Augustine and Chrysostom. The former guides his theological perspective, while the latter shapes his exegetical method.[6] This is clear in the number of times he cites Augustine in the *Institutes* over Chrysostom, and the reverse in his commentaries.[7] The primary methodological distinctions that they offer crystalise in the fact that he composes a hermeneutical-dogmatic treatise and commentaries separately. This stands in opposition particularly to the work of his contemporary, Martin Bucer, who supplied his own commentaries with lengthy dogmatic discussions that often detract the focus from the biblical book under investigation. At the same time, his exegetical attention in his commentaries varied from the selective brevity of Philip Melanchthon's *Loci communes* that considered only central topics of a biblical book.[8]

Against these, Calvin separated dogmatic discussions and biblical exegesis, though he did not sever the ties between the two.[9] He published the *Institutes* first to avoid doctrinal asides in his commentaries, but also with the intent that it function as a *hermeneutical guide* that would prepare

---

5. Gilmont, *John Calvin*, 114-15.

6. Holder is emphatic about the dual-influence of these Fathers within the commentaries, arguing that Augustine guided Calvin's *hermeneutical principles*, while Chrysostom governed his *rules of exegesis* (Holder, "Calvin as commentator," 251-52). Following the discovery of Calvin's annotated copy of the 1536 Latin edition of Chrysostom's Works, Ganoczy has demonstrated the Reformer's immediate access to the Church Father. For a hermeneutical analysis of the annotations, including his notes on Chrysostom's third homily on 2 Thessalonians, see Ganoczy and Müller, *Calvins handschriftliche Annotationen*, esp. 133-36. For the edition possessed by Calvin, see Desiderius Erasmus, *Divi Chrysostomi*.

7. Citations alone are not sufficient. This argument also bears in mind the number of times Calvin cites or utilizes the respective Fathers *positively*. See Walchenbach, *Calvin as Biblical Commentator*, 24-28, 47-49; Hazlett, "Calvin's Latin Preface," 129-150.

8. Calvin draws this distinction himself in the dedication of his first commentary (Romans). Calvin, *Epistles of Paul*, 2-3; Parker, *Calvin's New Testament Commentaries*, 51-54; Thompson, "Calvin as a Biblical Interpreter," 61-62.

9. Steinmetz, *Calvin in Context*, 13.

Receiving 2 Thessalonians

students for reading the Bible.[10] This helpfully limits the breadth of doctrinal discussion in his commentaries.

A few comments will help situate our understanding of the *Institutes* as it relates to 2 Thessalonians. The *Institutes* intentionally differs from the works of his contemporaries and is divided into four books, corresponding roughly to the four parts of the Apostles' Creed: (1) God the Creator, (2) Christ the redeemer, (3) the mediation of the grace of Christ,[11] and (4) the holy catholic church (including discussions of the sacraments and civil government). The majority of 2 Thessalonians citations fall in the third and fourth books. In the case of the former, the majority are from 2 Thess 1 and relate to the reception of Christ's grace. For the latter, most citations come from 2 Thess 2 and relate in some way to the approaching fullness of God's kingdom. Those verses relating to Church discipline (3:6–15) are also primarily found in the fourth book, which follows with its structure. Citations elsewhere in the *Institutes* are largely from the second chapter of 2 Thessalonians.

He structures his 2 Thessalonians commentary similarly to his other Pauline commentaries, and decidedly different from his law and gospel harmonies. Like many of his predecessors, this commentary opens with an *argumentum*. Similar to Chrysostom and Haimo, Calvin comments on select lemmas and proceeds through each verse of the book.

Calvin suggests that Paul wrote the letter from Athens in order to prevent the Thessalonians from feeling he had neglected them by not visiting them on his return to Jerusalem. This does not appropriately address the apparent seriousness of issues raised in the epistle, not to mention the verbal overlap with 1 Thessalonians, which modern scholars equate with pseudonymity or evidence of its authorship soon after the first epistle. It is also an odd departure from his predecessors, who emphasise the theological concerns as motivation for its writing. After this, Calvin summarizes the content as an exhortation to patience (chapter 1), a correction to the belief that Christ's return was imminent (chapter 2), and dealing with the idle (chapter 3).

---

10. Calvin makes this point in an explanation prefixed to the *Institutes*. See Calvin, *Institutes*, 1:4–5; Holder, "Calvin as Commentator," 232–35; de Greef, "Calvin's Writings," 44–45.

11. The term "roughly" applies to this book especially, because it lacks the "Holy Spirit" in its title and the resurrection appears here, instead of in book 4, where one would expect to find it.

The Reformation

In commenting on the text itself, Calvin divides the chapters into digestible sections (1:1-7a, 7b-10, 11-12; 2:1-2, 3-4, 5-8, 9-12, 13-14, 15-17; 3:1-5, 6-10, 11-13, 14-18), and comments on nearly every verse. As his *argumentum* indicates, this entails an emphasis on encouragement in chapter 1, primarily by directing the readers toward the eschatological assurances of God (i.e., the reversal of fortunes (1:5-9) and glorification with the Lord (1:10-12)).

Calvin's reading of chapter 2 differs from his preterist reading of Daniel, in which he sees the references to different beasts as a prophecy extending from Babylon to the Roman Empire, and therefore located entirely in the past.[12] In 2 Thess 2, Calvin sees an inaugurated prophecy awaiting fulfilment in the future, which he expected was not too distant. The "man of sin" (2:3), again, is Antichrist, but in a manner closer to Augustine than Chrysostom, this figure is a "body," rather than an individual, which Calvin equates with the preeminent and continuing leadership of the papacy. Therefore the "temple of God" (2:4) must be the Church for Calvin. The only thing that "restrains" (2:6) Antichrist was the sending of the gospel to the Gentiles, which has already taken place. The destruction of Antichrist (i.e., the papacy and his adherents) comes about through the "breath of [the Lord Jesus'] mouth" (2:8), which Calvin equates with the active preaching of God's word. Therefore the victory does not come about in a grand cosmic battle, but gradually through continued proclamation until truth completely vanquishes its enemy. At some point, Christ himself will arrive. Calvin never hesitates to assert that all of this comes about according to the preordained work of God.

The final chapter offers a preliminary excursus on the nature of faith (3:1-2) before focusing on the treatment of the "ἄτακτος" (3:6). Calvin considers this "disorderliness" a form of laziness that results from not considering the purpose for which humanity was created (i.e., to glorify God). It includes a wide range of people, especially certain poor individuals and monastics as a whole, or so it seems. For Calvin, this chapter offers directions for excommunication, which he sees extending to casual contact and the reception of communion, but not to hearing the preaching of the gospel.

---

12. See the translator's preface and Calvin's comments in Calvin, *Commentaries on Daniel*, xxxvi-xxxix, 186-87, respectively. In this volume, Calvin does not cite 2 Thessalonians.

Influential Impulses for Interpreting 2 Thessalonians

A number of influences come to a head in Calvin's reading of 2 Thessalonians, most notably his humanist attention to rhetoric and attention to primary sources.[13] Calvin sets aside the spiritual interpretations of his predecessors that undermine the plain sense of the text. Therefore, patristic works no longer held the same weight of authority that they had for previous generations, like the Carolingians.[14] His rhetorical training also means that he considers the effect(s) the letter may have on its readers. In general, this leads us to consider the *practicality* of Calvin in his work,[15] which may stem from his rhetorical and legal education, the manner in which he modelled his work after and had a career similar to John Chrysostom,[16] from the influence of Paul, his bias against scholastic methods and theology, his nominalist leanings, or all of the above. Regardless of the source(s), the practical emphasis of Calvin is readily noticeable, colouring even his doctrinal considerations. For this reason, we attend first to the hermeneutical role of practical, pastoral concern in Calvin's reception of 2 Thessalonians.

Another impulse that guides Calvin's reading of the epistle is his theological framework reflected in the *Institutes* and deployed in his other writings. Therefore, three key theological themes are the focus of our discussion following Calvin's practicality: divine sovereignty, ecclesiology, and eschatology. Connected with this final theological concept is the influence of the papacy, the Roman Church, and the Reformation milieu on his reading of 2 Thessalonians, all of which receive attention in the final section

---

13. As T. F. Torrance has shown, Calvin's humanist training had a decidedly Parisian influence through the earlier work of John Duns Scotus, William of Occam, and John Major Haddington. See Torrance, *Hermeneutics of John Calvin*, 3–57.

14. Lane has published a detailed study of Calvin's use of the Fathers within the framework of eleven theses. Of particular note are theses II (Calvin's use of the Fathers "is primarily a polemical appeal to authorities"), III ("Calvin is less interested in authorities but instead debates with other interpreters"), and IV (negative remarks about a patristic source "may be a mark of respect") (Lane, *John Calvin*, esp. 1–13). See also Steinmetz, "Calvin and the Patristic Exegesis of Paul," 116–18.

15. Dowey speaks of "Calvin's soteriological focus on 'useful' and 'practical' knowledge—'useful' for savlation and 'practical' for the Christian life" (Dowey, *Knowledge of God*, 248). Similarly, Placher argues that Calvin uses the doctrine of predestination "to obtain practical results in the affections and actions of believers" (Placher, *Domestication of Transcendence*, 54).

16. Walchenbach, *Calvin as Biblical Commentator*, 21; Thompson, "Calvin as a Biblical Interpreter," 63.

THE PRACTICAL PASTOR

Calvin's practicality cannot be overemphasised. Regarding predestination, he says the doctrine "builds up faith soundly, trains us to humility, elevates us to admiration of the immense goodness of God towards us, and excites us to praise his goodness."[17] He is prone to practical, rather than speculative, consideration of any doctrine.

Calvin's practical-pastoral concern materializes as asides and exegetical maneuvers that he makes within the commentaries.[18] "Pastoral concern" has a generic ring to it, therefore, we might clarify that this concern has primarily to do with shaping his readers into pious, obedient Christians generally through drawing universally applicable conclusions from the text. The practical-pastoral emphases flow from the content of the epistle, and therefore resist categorization. So, we proceed with Calvin through the letter. In order to give a picture of Calvin's practicality and to avoid redundancy, here we look at 1 Thess 1 and 3, while reserving discussion of chapter 2[19] for the final section of this chapter on the papacy and the Antichrist

Practical Concerns: 2 Thessalonians 1

His pastoral concern appears first in his comment on the opening thanksgiving (1:3), in which he takes Paul's obligation to give thanks for the growth of the Thessalonians in faith and love as having dual implications for Christians. From the perspective of the letter's recipients, Calvin points out that "the godly should all hold to the principle of examining themselves each day and seeing the extent of their progress," adding "Our own leisureliness is all the more disgraceful when we hardly move a single foot

---

17. Calvin, *Concerning the Eternal Predestination*, 56.

18. Holder adds that Calvin's rhetorical style in the commentaries is shaped by this pastoral concern. See Holder, "Calvin as Commentator," 243. Elsewhere, he recognizes the centrality of the congregation to Calvin's hermeneutic. In Calvin's theology, he argues: "The congregation functions as a 'community of discourse'—the communal context in which particular textual readings come to have meaning" (Holder, "Ecclesia," 277–78; cf. Calvin, *Institutes* 4.1.9).

19. Calvin's practical emphases in 2 Thess 2 generally have to do with *encouraging* his readers that that (1) they have revealed knowledge of the Last Days, (2) to persevere in the faith in persecution, and (3) to hold in their minds the secured future of Christ's unending reign.

over a protracted period."[20] The specific content of Paul's praise becomes a challenge to Christians in general.

He then looks at the verse from the apostle's position, perceiving his response as exemplary, and exhorts his readers: "Whenever the goodness of God shines forth, it is fitting that we should show appreciation of it. Then too, the well-being of our brethren ought to be of such concern to us that we reckon among our own blessings any blessing that has been bestowed on them."[21] Thus, instruction in godly living is drawn from both *what* Paul praises and *the reason for his thanksgiving*.

In the next verse, as Paul commends the Thessalonians for their patience and faith in their persecutions (1:4), he implicitly encourages faithfulness in his readers by observing, "There is nothing . . . that sustains us in tribulation as faith does, and this truth is sufficiently clear from the fact that as soon as we cease to be aware of the promises of God, we completely fail."[22] In this case, the example of the Thessalonians, as recorded by Paul, gives a lasting and certain theological truth that warns against neglecting the promises of God.

When considering the partial, present signs of God's judgment to come (1:5–6), which indicate his restraint from judging in the present, Calvin regards this as profound instruction for the character of the Christian "mind."[23] This heuristic text directs Christians away from security in the world and the hopelessness in suffering to the certain future in which God exercises his office as Judge.

He argues similarly in the *Institutes* that the sufferings of Christians as the just judgment of God, which lead to their being "counted worthy" (1:5), are qualified by the verses that follow, so that they are not to "prove that works have any worth but to strengthen hope in God's Kingdom."[24] With our minds shaped in this way, Calvin confidently asserts, "Death will thus be for us the image of life."[25]

---

20. Calvin, *Epistles of Paul*, 387–88.

21. Calvin, *Epistles of Paul*, 388.

22. Calvin, *Epistles of Paul*, 388.

23. "Insignis certe locus, quia docet quemadmodum excitandae sint *mentes* nostrae ab omnibus mundi obstaculis" (Calvin, *Comm. 2 Thess* [CO 52:189]).

24. Calvin, *Institutes* 3.18.7.

25. Calvin, *Epistles of Paul*, 390.

On 1:4, Cajetan reiterates that the boasting of Paul is due to the increased faith and love of the Thessalonians,[26] but his reading is purely descriptive. Estius generally follows Cajetan, though he adds that the example encourages the larger Church (to endure persecution?).[27] In so doing, Estius has incorporated a fourth perspective in the discussion. Including Calvin's comments, we have the view of the apostle, the first recipients, and the third-party "churches" to which Paul refers. All of these perspectives work together to draw out subtly varying dimensions of the text's meaning(s) for the present Church.

At 1:5–6, Zwingli comments extensively, primarily with a pastoral interest in resolving the theodical issues presented by the verses. He compresses the ἔνδειγμα of God's just judgment into two points illuminated by his sending persecutions: the persecutions test the good as a means of preparing them for their future life in the kingdom and they give reason for God to punish the wicked, who afflicted the righteous.[28] Given his precursory role in the Reformation, Zwingli's similar stance to Calvin indicates that, though Calvin's reading might mature from his own theology, his reading is aesthetically neutral within the horizon of expectations of his time. This is not to critique Calvin for lacking creativity. Indeed, it would be suspicious if Calvin presented revolutionary readings at every single verse. If anything, this may confirm the veracity of the reading, given its historical legacy.

Calvin's interpretation stands in stark contrast to Estius, who sees the patient suffering of the righteous as *meriting* eternal glory, rather than serving as an indication of God's election. In a rare move, Estius openly challenges a "heresy of Calvin and the other sects of our time" with a two point argument from 2 Thess 1:5–6. In the first case, he asserts that God purges believers presently by allowing or inflicting them with persecutions and tribulations. This is the primary purgative means of preparing them to enter the kingdom of God.[29] Secondly, because their endurance renders them worthy, their entry into the kingdom must be considered, in some part,

---

26. Cajetan, *Epistolae Pauli*, 136.

27. "Ut nos ipsi de vobis gloriemur apud alias Ecclesias Dei, vestro exemplo cohortantes caeteros" (Estius, *In omnes D. Pauli*, 571).

28. "Duplici ergo ratione dominus persequutiones mittit idque iusto iudicio. Primum et boni per ignem probentur. Secundo ut mali puniatur, et sic declaretur iustum iudicium dei" (Zwingli, "In ii. epist. ad Thess," 239).

29. Estius points to the purity of the gold stones of the heavenly city (Rev 21:21) as evidence for the ongoing need for believers to be purified (Estius, *In omnes D. Pauli*, 742).

as due to their merit and not grace *alone*. The "evidence of the righteous judgment of God" (1:5) is that he has withdrawn eternal punishment and allows the purifying, temporal punishment.[30] In this case, the two readings cannot be resolved as "standing in tension" with one another. One must be correct and the other false.

Considering God's future act of "rendering vengeance" (1:8), Calvin resolves theodical issues of suffering in the present, then turns to ask "whether it is lawful for us to seek revenge, because Paul promises revenge as something that may rightfully be sought?"[31] It appears that he anticipates this question only a sentence earlier when he describes vengeance as the eschatological "office" enjoined to Christ by God. Therefore, he concludes that vengeance belongs to the Lord and that Christians must not pursue vengeance because: they must seek the good of all people and they might long for vengeance rendered on the wicked, but "wicked" is an eschatological category, and we lack the knowledge of who these wicked are in advance of the eschaton.[32] Therefore, vengeance belongs to the Lord.[33]

Our final example of pastoral concern in 2 Thess 1 comes in an attempt by Calvin to ground the verse in the experience of his congregants. Paul prays that God fulfil "every work of faith, with power" (1:11), which turns Calvin's attention to the weakness of humans. This affords him the opportunity to remind his readers of the helplessness of people, when left on their own, so that they require divine "power" to make possible any "work of faith" (1:11). Calvin's purpose is to encourage his readers to come to terms with the Divine reality that undergirds them.[34] As our section on rhetoric has shown, Calvin constantly directs the gaze of his readers God-ward in the hope that repetition will drive the point home and affect a consistent, satisfactory rest in the gracious sovereignty of God.

Luther enters the discussion at 1:8 in his commentary on Genesis 49:1-2 using language common to the discussion[35] of God's patient endurance of wickedness so that he may justly inflict vengeance on those who

30. Estius, *In omnes D. Pauli*, 742; cf. Thiselton, *1 and 2 Thessalonians*, 203.

31. Calvin, *Epistles of Paul*, 392.

32. Calvin, *Epistles of Paul*, 391-92.

33. "Porro hoc ad Christum refertur, qui reddet ultionem. Significat enim Paulus, has illi a Deo patre iniunctas esse partes" (Calvin, *Comm. 2 Thess* [CO 52:191]).

34. In this way, Calvin approaches Chrysostom's emphasis that his congregants constantly engage with the truths of scripture and that they become aware of the Divine presence in the reading of scripture.

35. cf. Zwingli, "In ii. epist. ad Thess," 239; Calvin, *Epistles of Paul*, 389.

perpetuated it. Looking at the example of Jacob, who believed the promises of God, Luther draws a contrast between the righteous and the wicked. The righteous are characterised by faith, which both "believe[s] and fear[s] things that are invisible,"[36] namely the future judgment pronounced by God. Thus 2 Thess 1:8 functions as a threat, which the righteous take to heart, "but the ungodly do not fear, do not believe, do not hope, and do not care about God."[37] The verse simultaneously warns the righteous and condemns the wicked. Calvin recognizes a distinction between the two groups of people (though that deserves fuller discussion in another section), yet he does not explore the manner in which this verse *speaks to* the righteous and the wicked. His concern regarding Christians exacting vengeance in the present applies generally like Luther's points, though it comes from asking about the parallel between the office(s) of the Lord and the manner in which his disciples must follow him.

With Luther, Cajetan emphasizes Christ's office as judge, reflecting a longstanding Christological tradition.[38] Calvin takes up the discussion, but poses the new question "How does Christ function as exemplar?" tempered by temporal considerations (i.e., the *eschaton* has not arrived). When turning to the "work of faith in power" (1:11), Cajetan looks primarily to the Lord as the source of "power" to sustain believers with the gift of faith in persecutions and tribulation.[39] Again, Calvin agrees, but where Cajetan looks primarily about how this reveals the gracious goodness of God, Calvin reads the weakness, or incapacity of people to accomplish anything apart from this gracious source.

Initially, Zwingli offers the same reading as Cajetan, but then he proposes an alternative, suggesting that it could mean: "that your faith might be able to work,"[40] so that faith would be genuine and verifiable by the fruits it produces. In this way, the verse becomes a means of determining the efficaciousness of God's grace in the individual. The absence of "working

---

36. Luther, *Commentary on Genesis* (LW 8:202).

37. Luther, *Commentary on Genesis* (LW 8:202).

38. "Participium dantis refertur ad domini iesu. Officium describitur ad quod exercendum veniet" (Cajetan, *Epistolae Pauli*, 136).

39. Cajetan, *Epistolae Pauli*, 137. Estius reads the passage similarly (Estius, *In omnes D. Pauli*, 3:573).

40. Zwingli, "In ii. epist. ad Thess," 241.

faith," which should illuminate "the name of our Lord Jesus Christ," indicates that a person has feigned belief.[41]

Practical Concerns: 2 Thessalonians 3

Calvin's overwhelming pastoral concern in 2 Thess 3 has to do with Church discipline. This discussion revolves around Paul's response to those who might disobey his injunction that all of the members of the Christian community must work (3:12). In his comments, we see the confluence of the text's effects and the receptive influences of Calvin's own context.[42] Regarding "effect," the discussion centralizes on addressing those who refuse to obey Christian instruction. Regarding "reception," however, we recognize Calvin's use of "excommunication" language and the relationship of rebellious individuals to the Church at large, rather than the specific community at Thessalonica.

Therefore, in connecting Paul's warning to any person who "does not obey our word" (3:14) with the fact that Paul has "no command but *from the Lord*" (cf. 2 Thess 3:6; 1 Thess 5:14; Cor 7:10),[43] is able to form a strong basis for the disciplinary action of excommunication. For those who openly rebel against God, Calvin argues that the Church must "point out their diseases to the physician [God?] whose task it is to heal them."[44] Furthermore, in having "no company with him" (2 Thess 3:14), the practice of excommunication treats with compulsion and brings into submission the rebellious, so that "they learn to obey."[45]

---

41. Zwingli, "In ii. epist. ad Thess," 241.

42. "The text-reader relation (i.e., effect as the element that is conditioned by the text and reception as the element of concretization of meaning that is conditioned by the addressee) must be distinguished, worked out, and mediated if one wishes to see how expectation and experience mesh and whether an element of new significance emerges" (Jauss, *Aesthetic Experience*, xxxii; cf. "Theory of Reception," 60).

43. Calvin, *Epistles of Paul*, 421. The referent is not exactly clear. It may allude to 2 Thess 3:6, but Paul does not say, "We have no command," but rather, "We command you." Additionally, the only portion of this phrase that is a direct quote in the Latin appears to be "ex Domino," which makes tracing the reference difficult. See Calvin, *Comm. 2 Thess* (CO 52:215). In point of fact, this comes close to Chrysostom's affirmation of scripture as "letters sent by God" noted in chapter 2 above.

44. Calvin, *Epistles of Paul*, 421.

45. Calvin, *Epistles of Paul*, 421.

To Paul's aim that the individual "be ashamed" (3:14) Calvin adds that it teaches them to obey the commands of Holy Scripture, that it stems the contamination of their rebellion in the Church, prevents disgracing the Church, and that the example functions as a warning to others. He concludes his review of this verse with the insight that excommunication functions as a "bridle" (*fraeno*)[46] for the already impudent, but it prevents that impudence from expanding. In this way, the text is not simply against the idle, but any wanton individual within the Church and it operates under Calvin's assumption of humanity's corruption.

Calvin's closing pastoral remark follows on Paul's own that the community "not regard him as an enemy, but warn him as a brother" (3:15). Again, like his theological predecessors (e.g., Chrysostom),[47] Calvin extends this practice as the general rule for Church discipline, and reminds his readers, "the intention of excommunication is not to drive men from the Lord's flock, but rather to bring them back again when they have wandered astray."[48] Calvin's concern, and the Church's at large, has expanded beyond a response to idleness to wilful rebellion within the Christian community. The dialogue is shaped by the text, but not without concerns stemming from the Reformation context.

In the *Institutes*, Calvin deals specifically with the Church's administration of discipline, relating every reference to 2 Thess 3:14–15 to excommunication, both in terms of its function and its application.[49] In one context, Calvin connects Paul's exhortation to Christ's declaration to Peter that whatever he "binds on earth will be bound in heaven" (Matt 18:18). Significantly, Calvin describes this as Christ's promise to the Church as "his people,"[50] rather than to Peter specifically, thereby withdrawing it from its longstanding location in the doctrine of papal authority. By bringing these texts together under the topic of excommunication, Calvin perceives this pronouncement by the Church as binding one to damnation, unless they should repent.

One of the earliest texts in which Calvin discusses excommunication, *Articles Concerning the Organization of the Church and of Worship at Geneva*, includes a similar appeal to Matt 18 (though not 2 Thess 3:14–15).

---

46. Calvin, *Comm. 2 Thess* (CO 52:216).
47. Cf. John Chrysostom, *In epist. ii ad Thess* 5 (PG 62:493). See also chapter 2 above.
48. Calvin, *Epistles of Paul*, 422.
49. Calvin, *Institutes* 4.1.26, 4.12.5.
50. Calvin, *Institutes* 4.12.10.

This writing reveals that, from the outset, Calvin insisted on the power of the Church as a body of believers and particularly the lay leadership of a congregation to enforce excommunication.[51]

It is not insignificant that Calvin consistently advances the role of the Church in pronouncing and enforcing excommunication in his later works. In his time at Geneva, Calvin came into conflict with the political council of the city on several occasions over the location of authority to enforce excommunication. The first wrangling over this topic with the Genevan Council in 1538, in part a response to the *Articles*, resulted in the expulsion of Calvin and Farel from the city.[52] Though he had no difficulty in wresting excommunication from the hands of the Catholics, the leaders of his own city believed that the excommunicative power belonged to the Council, rather than the Church. The Church could pass a judgment, but enforcement belonged to civil authorities.

It is in this context that the nature of excommunication for Calvin and the Reformers becomes clear: it has to do primarily with the refusal to allow an individual participation in Holy Communion and only secondarily with the withdrawal of casual association. How could civil authorities prevent an excommunicant from receiving the Eucharist or force a pastor to administer the same? The issue arose again after Calvin's return to Geneva in 1543, prior to the authorship of his commentary. A decade later, the execution of excommunication became the focal point during the tumult over Servetus (1553), and later that same year with Philibert Berthelier for public drunkenness.[53] Thus, the discussion of excommunication in the *Institutes* under the topic of Church is decidedly pointed for Calvin, and he has to carefully strike a balance between taking the authority from the papacy without giving it to the civil magistrates in a Christian society.

Martin Luther's "Sermon on the Ban" is dedicated specifically to the administration and function of excommunication. Like Calvin, he finds the source for its administration in Matt 18, but articulates various dimensions not found in Calvin's work. For instance, Luther speaks of two forms of excommunication (*der Bann*),[54] an inward one by which God withdraws

51. Calvin, *Theological Treatises*, 47–53.
52. Ozment, *Age of Reform*, 362.
53. de Greef, *Writings of John Calvin*, 43–45.
54. Luther demonstrates the philological dimension of excommunication by pointing out to his congregation that Christians participate in "communio" (fellowship) with one another. The opposite of this concept, "excommunicatio," entails exclusion from fellowship. See Luther, "Ein Sermon von dem Bann" (WA 6:63).

spiritual communion from the rebellious individual and which cannot be implemented by the Church, and outward excommunication, which the Church administers and which revokes their access to Christian fellowship.

The second form of excommunication is divided into a smaller ban and a larger one, both of which are given by Jesus. The smaller ban is the revocation of fellowship between individuals when one sins against another (Matt 18:15), while the larger ban follows on from the smaller if the impudent individual refuses to repent after being confronted by a group of two or three witnesses. This larger ban involves cessation from Christian fellowship. Luther substantiates his definition of excommunication with Paul's warning "If anyone refuses to obey what we say in this letter . . . have nothing to do with him, that he may be ashamed" (2 Thess 3:14).

In the larger context, Luther is railing against the arbitrary implementation and abuse of excommunication by Catholic Church authorities. By transferring "true" excommunication to the hands of God, Luther diminishes the authority of the Church with the hope of stemming abuse. Furthermore, as the aim of excommunication entails repentance, Luther insists that the individual under "the ban" be allowed to attend church services in order that they might hear the gospel. The rebellious person will be refused communion, but no one may deny him/her the spiritual sacrament through which God may speak and which God alone may revoke.[55]

Interestingly, Luther says nothing about the relationship of the text from 2 Thessalonians to those who do not work—the historical addressees of Paul. Calvin discusses a theorised historical context, which includes those who refuse to work, but locates the meaning of the text in his own horizon in applying the ecclesial tool of excommunication. The text offers a great deal more in a context where doctrine has been built upon key texts, such as 2 Thess 3:14-15. Green's observation is fitting here regarding the change in emphasis from the historical setting of the letter to the Reformation: "Scripture-formed patterns of thinking and acting might take different

---

55. Luther, "Ein Sermon von dem Bann" (WA 6:63–75). Luther argues similarly, but briefly in the Smalcald Articles (2.9; ca. 1537). Zwingli offers a congruent assertion in his Sixty-Seven Theses (31–32; ca. 1523), as does the Anabaptist Balthasar Hubmaier in *Christian Catechism* (ca. 1526), and Elizabeth I in the Thirty-Nine Articles (33; ca. 1563), thereby reflecting a trend in the Reformation to decentralise a particular power once concentrated in the hands of a few. See Janz, *Reformation Reader*, 136, 157, 175–76, 322, respectively.

shapes—not because the words of Scripture have changed, but because the social contexts within which those words are read and put into play vary."[56]

Cajetan reads Paul's exhortation not to "weary in doing good" (3:13) as a reminder to the readers not to cease in giving alms and, like Calvin, the final verses (3:14–15) provides a basis for the doctrine of excommunication, which has to do mainly with the abrogation of common fellowship.[57]

Situating the chapter in the larger context of the epistle, namely Paul's encouragement to a persecuted group, Zwingli understands the exhortation not to "weary in doing good" (3:13) as a reminder to a group that would be challenged to do so under the weight of numerous afflictions. To the conversation of excommunication, Zwingli adds, "Even if you withdraw from [the excommunicant] physically . . . embrace them in mind, love them."[58]

Estius speaks of the closing verses (3:14–15) as a description of "ecclesiastical discipline,"[59] which Paul will enforce, but then cites and follows Cajetan's perspective on excommunication, which belongs ultimately to the papacy.

In his locating excommunication in the Church as a holistic body, rather than a particular leader, Calvin satisfies the horizon of expectation established by Luther. He surpasses it, though, in asking how this relates to civil Christian governments and he renders the program more "democratic."

Two observations might be drawn from the reception history of this text: first, from an early date the Church has shifted from reading this text primarily with regard to "idlers" who disobey Paul's instruction to Christians in general who cause a disturbance in the community through wilful iniquity. Second, the term "excommunication" is conspicuously absent from many modern commentaries,[60] perhaps because it is seen as anachronistic.

The fading of Luther and Calvin's questions likely has to do with the decreased animosity between Catholic and Protestant scholars, who already assume how excommunication should be practiced in their own communities. Dialogue with this passage shifted from how the Church should implement discipline with an assumption about who had the authority to

---

56. Green, *Seized by Truth*, 20.

57. Cajetan, *Epistolae Pauli*, 138–39. Both authors make reference to the poor either explicitly or implicitly, thereby revealing an influential reading that dates at least to Chrysostom.

58. Zwingli, "In ii. epist. ad Thess," 248.

59. Estius, *In omnes D. Pauli*, 758.

60. Exceptions include Best, *Thessalonians*, 344; Wanamaker, *Thessalonians*, 289, both of whom use the term sparingly.

do so (early Church–medieval Church), to questions that accepted the former point while reconsidering the latter assumption (the Reformation), to modern (Western) questions that also accept the passage's instruction for Church discipline in general, yet they mature from a fractious society oriented toward the individual. In many cases, the abundance of denominations resulted from rebellion against the excommunicative regulations that the Reformers attempted to put in place. The newer questions do not negate the Reformers', but depict a priority based on the more immediate need.

THEOLOGICAL EXEGESIS

Diverging slightly from the pattern of investigation set above, we turn our attention to another critical receptive dimension of Calvin's interaction with 2 Thessalonians: the doctrinal/theological "tools"[61] that shape his reading of the letter. This section concentrates primarily on giving a coherent picture of Calvin's theological reading of 2 Thessalonians without engaging with his contemporaries.

Calvin interprets within a decidedly explicit theological framework that mutually shapes and is shaped by his reading of 2 Thessalonians. Of particular interest with regard to this epistle are Calvin's reading according to his theological conceptions of divine sovereignty, ecclesiology, and eschatology. Again, this doctrinal reading is not to be taken as comprehensive of Calvin's thought. Instead, it is an attempt to determine those factors that guide his dialogue with the text and lead to a "Calvinist" meaning in a sixteenth-century context.

Divine Sovereignty

Marking the transition within the thanksgiving section (1:3–2:12) from the thanksgiving proper (1:3–4) to the first stage of parenesis (1:5–10),[62] Calvin determines that the "manifest token of the righteous judgment of God" (1:5) should be taken as "the wrongs and persecutions which the innocent suffer at the hands of rogues and criminals clearly show that one day God

---

61. For this language and an evaluation of the theological nature of Calvin's exegesis, see Gamble, "Calvin as Theologian," 53–54, 58–60.
62. For this outline, see Malherbe, *Letters to the Thessalonians*, ix.

will be judge of the world."[63] This flies in the face of contemporary perspectives that the path of history is a result of chance and it implies God has no control therein,[64] perspectives due to the "unredeemed mind," and Calvin offers a reading to combat such a position. The sovereignty of God is seen explicitly in the suffering of the righteous and the afflictive power of the persecutors, because in that scenario God points to the reversal of fortunes in the future.

As the first chapter concludes, Calvin notes that Paul could have ended with the prayer that the Thessalonians' faith be fulfilled by God (1:12), but he adds "good pleasure" (*beneplacitum*).[65] That is to say, "God was persuaded by nothing other than His own goodness"[66] to bring about salvation in his elect. We might helpfully add to this category of sovereignty the influence of Calvin's doctrine of grace on his reading, for shortly after the above argument, he adds that the whole of our salvation belongs to the "pure grace of God," unassisted by good works.[67] Calvin's rewording of the phrase "that our God may . . . [fulfill] every work of faith" (1:12) as "that your faith may be fulfilled" (*ut impleatur fides vestra*)[68] renders his perspective unambiguous. God is not just fulfilling hypothetical/potential "works of faith," but the very faith of the individual in his sovereignty.

Barth traces Calvin's view of grace in the Middle Ages to Duns Scotus, who reckoned that only God's grace renders works meritorious in any capacity.[69] Though Calvin may have encountered this dimension of Scotus's theology during his time in Paris, it most likely reached Calvin later, filtered

---

63. Calvin, *Epistles of Paul*, 388. Though Calvin insists that he omits "any reference to the interpretations of other commentators" at this point, he clearly shares the perspective of Chrysostom. See John Chrysostom, *In epist. ii ad Thess* 2 (PG 62:475).

64. Wendel observes the relocation of Calvin's discussion of providence in the 1559 edition of the *Institutes* to just after his doctrine of creation. The close proximity of the topics emphasizes that "God is the Creator of the world: but having once created it he remains its absolute master, takes interest in it, intervenes in it at every moment, and abandons none of his power to the blind play of natural laws, still less to chance" (Wendel, *Calvin*, 177).

65. Calvin, *Comm. 2 Thess* (CO 52:193).

66. Calvin, *Epistles of Paul*, 394.

67. Calvin, *Epistles of Paul*, 394.

68. Calvin, *Comm. 2 Thess* (CO 52:193).

69. Barth, *Theology of John Calvin*, 34.

through the lens of Luther, who contended similarly, but insisted on the *active nature* of grace within the sovereign activity of God.[70]

Of "the one who now restrains" (ὁ κατέχων; 2:7) Calvin remarks that this indicates the temporary reign of Antichrist, whose limits "have been predetermined by God."[71] In the present and during the period of tribulation of Antichrist, "the breath of [Christ's] mouth" and the "appearance of his coming" (2:8) are euphemistic expressions for the gift of Christ's spiritual presence through the preaching of the gospel, which God has given to keep the elect safe from "all the wiles of Satan."[72] As the chapter proceeds, Calvin looks again to God's provision for the elect by limiting Satan's power over "them that are perishing" (2:10). This only further confirms the limited power of Satan and Antichrist, which they have through divine permission.[73]

Shortly thereafter, Calvin engages in the theodical debate of whether those "who did not receive the love of the truth" (2:10) extends only to those who wilfully reject the gospel, or also to those have never heard its message. He concludes, "My answer is that this particular judgment of God by which he has punished open defiance does not prevent Him from striking with wonder those who have never heard a single word about Christ as often as He wills."[74] He quickly follows this point, however, with the observation that this is not the focus of Paul's discussion. In so doing, Calvin attempts to forcefully close off questions generated in the historical dialogue with the text.

On the same passage in his other works, Calvin's discussion revolves around the relationship of Satan to God and the nature of election. In the *Institutes*, for example, Calvin repeatedly insists that the activity of the lawless one and the deception of the perishing (2:9-10) take place under the permissive control of God. Satan, in fact, is compelled to do the bidding of God, for though he is rebellious in will, he cannot help but accomplish the will of God.[75] Calvin determines this from the fact that the discussion concludes with God sending the "strong delusion" (2:11). Thus he avers

---

70. Barth, *Theology of John Calvin*, 42-43. See, Luther, *Disputatio contra scholasticum theologiam. 1517* (WA 1:225-28).

71. Calvin, *Epistles of Paul*, 404.

72. Calvin, *Epistles of Paul*, 405.

73. Calvin, *Epistles of Paul*, 406.

74. Calvin, *Epistles of Paul*, 407.

75. Calvin, *Institutes* 1.14.17.

that the individual is the author of his/her own just vengeance, Satan is the minister of it, and God sends the delusion,[76] such that "Satan intervenes to stir up the reprobate whenever the Lord by his providence destines them to one end or another."[77] God uses both the wicked and Satan as instruments to accomplish his will.

In response to this reading of 2 Thessalonians, Calvin must elsewhere defend himself against the position that God is the author of sin[78] and the predestination of the reprobate. The first point he addressed in a tractate against Castellio entitled *Brief Reply in Refutation of the Calumnies of a Certain Worthless Person*. He begins with the assertion that God gives Satan the power to delude the reprobate (2:11) as well as sending a lying spirit to the prophets of Ahab for his deception (1 Kings 22:22). Therefore, Satan operates under the licence of God. For Calvin, the issue is primarily a matter of will. Both Satan and God may will the destruction of an individual, but Satan does so for corrupt purposes, while God does so for the greater purpose of his infinitely deep, providential purposes for the world. Thus the destruction of that individual may come about, but Satan, in seeking his own will, has accomplished the will of God under his permission.[79] This is strikingly reminiscent of Haimo.

Regarding the predestination of the reprobate, Calvin first undergirds his doctrine of the predestination of the elect with the God's choice of the elect to salvation and sanctification "from the beginning" (ἀπ' ἀρχῆς; 2 Thess 2:13).[80] Addressing his opponent Georgius of Sicily, who leaned toward universalism,[81] Calvin makes use of the same biblical texts as Georgius to refute his position. Taking up 2 Thess 2:13 again, Calvin rejects his opponent's position that predestination has anything to do with "being born at a certain time," as this overlooks the emphases on salvation and sanctification in the verse, and he argues that it clearly points to the

---

76. Calvin, *Institutes* 1.18.2.

77. Calvin, *Institutes* 2.4.5.

78. For Calvin and his predecessors, predestination and free will operate on two different causal levels. Secondly, sin itself is not "caused," and is thereby irrational, which maintains the shocking reality of sin as rebellion against God's will. This behavior does not then fall outside of the realm of God's "control," but functions as a mystery in which the causal join between "sin" and God's ordering of history remains a mystery. See Placher, *Domestication of Transcendence*, 210–11.

79. Calvin, *Institutes* 1.18.2.

80. Calvin, *Concerning the Eternal Predestination*, 105.

81. See Reid's introduction in Calvin, *Concerning the Eternal Predestination*, 11.

preferential election of some over others.⁸² If we recall from the previous chapter on Haimo, Calvin's double-predestination falls outside of the sanctioned perspective of predestination within the Medieval Church, enlisting 2 Thess 2:11 as demonstrable of God's election of the reprobate.⁸³

Calvin transfers from this topic to the preservation of the elect, as it materializes in the closing thanksgiving of the section (2:13). Again, preferring the reading "God chose you from the beginning" (2:13), Calvin determines that Paul means Satan never threatens the salvation of the elect, which God has established "before the creation of the world."⁸⁴ He adds that we have no business attempting to penetrate the secret counsel of God, either for the reasoning behind his election, or as to whether one is elected.⁸⁵ Instead, he concludes that God offers outward tokens of his election to give believers confidence. For Calvin, the presence of the Spirit in the individual's life, which leads to ever-deepening faith and regeneration, is a guard against those who might use his doctrine as a licence for licentiousness.⁸⁶

In Paul's benedictory prayer, in which he speaks of "the Lord of peace" (3:16), Calvin forwards part of his understanding of Christian prayer. Of significance is that the reference to peace indicates that the offering and maintenance of peace belongs to God.⁸⁷

A final note on divine sovereignty focuses on the preservation of this epistle and connects the latter two chapters of the letter. In response to Paul's apparent comment about pseudonymous epistles (2:2), Calvin offers thanks to God for keeping spurious documents out of the canon and preserving the authentic materials and concludes, "This certainly could not have taken place by chance or human effort, if God himself had not held Satan and all his ministers in check by His power."⁸⁸ Calvin recognizes this

---

82. Calvin, *Concerning the Eternal Predestination*, 159.

83. Calvin, *Theological Treatises*, 157, 175.

84. Calvin, *Epistles of Paul*, 409.

85. Steinmetz addresses this topic with attention to the debate over the absolute and ordained powers of God, part of which he sees clarified in relation to Calvin's views of providence and predestination (Steinmetz, *Calvin in Context*, 40–52).

86. Calvin, *Epistles of Paul*, 409–10.

87. Calvin, *Epistles of Paul*, 422.

88. Calvin, *Epistles of Paul*, 397. Had Calvin access to the Nag Hammadi library, their divergence from the canonical NT would render his view of divine sovereignty stronger.

security as well in the signature offered at the letter's conclusion (3:17), determining that its preservation is due to the "singular kindness of God."[89]

Though debate frequently concentrates on Calvin's view of predestination, his reading of 2 Thessalonians according to the guiding doctrine of divine sovereignty reveals a richer understanding of the dimensions of this element of his theology. God's sovereignty extends to the fulfilment of faith in the elect as well as their preservation through any tribulation, it limits Antichrist and Satan in time and permission, includes double-predestination, reaches those who have never heard the gospel, asserts God's continually active role in creation, and secured the preservation of sacred scriptures for the Church.[90]

Ecclesiology

Connected to this theological reading of two kingdoms is Calvin's advancement of the nature of the Church. The "true" Church is unified by spiritual bonds across congregations, though it does not attach every congregant to the life of God, as we have noted above. In general terms, the body of the Reformer's work has primarily to do with the Church, aiming to explicate the mysteries of God for the average Christian reader, unite those readers by dogmatic considerations, and lead to a way of life consistent with the ethical impulses of scripture.

Looking specifically at 2 Thessalonians, however, Calvin's primary focus with regard to the Church is articulation of its nature. Both the content of the epistle (i.e., the dualisms of wicked and righteous) and his historical context (i.e., the papacy as "the wicked" and the Church, as rearticulated by the Reformers, as "the righteous") nurture this reading. The latter in particular necessitates attention in this regard for Calvin, as he must both legitimate his abscission from the Roman Church and reveal the continuity of his "tradition" with the historical Church. This sets the stage for his reading of 2 Thessalonians within which the latter justification especially absorbs his interest.

We will avoid repeating the discussion of kingdoms and concentrate here on explicit references to the Church's nature and function. In the commentary and the *Institutes*, Calvin clusters the majority of his attention on

89. Calvin, *Epistles of Paul*, 423.

90. For the influence of Augustine on Calvin with regard to divine sovereignty, but particularly on his view of predestination, see Warfield, *Calvin and Augustine*.

the topic of the Church in the final chapter of the letter. This should not obscure his larger view of the Church, however, that comes to bear on his reading of 2 Thessalonians. Outside of chapter 3, Calvin offers only an observation regarding the Church in response to Paul's obligatory thanksgiving for the growth of the Thessalonians faith and love (1:3). Calvin considers these developments as due to God's goodness, adding, "If we consider the nature and holiness of the unity of Christ's body, there will be such a sharing in common amongst us that we shall consider the benefits enjoyed by every member to be the advantage of the whole Church. Consequently, in extolling the kindnesses of God we must always have regard to the whole Church."[91]

Superficially, this describes the appropriate response of the Church to any good experienced in the wider "body." Close attention here, however, reveals Calvin's view of the body of Christ and the two natures of Christ. For Calvin, Christ is undoubtedly present in the Christian community by his Holy Spirit, but, because his *physical* body suffers the spatial limitations of all other physical bodies, it can only be located in one place at any given time. Given the past occurrence of the ascension, therefore, Christ is *physically* present only in heaven. His *spiritual* nature is not limited thus and can pervade numerous regions.

This exploration of the natures of Christ, as manifest in the Church, becomes the particular focus in Calvin's understanding of Holy Communion.[92] He battles against the Catholic doctrine of transubstantiation and negotiates with the Zwinglians[93] an agreement over Communion. He perceives himself not as developing a radically new perspective, but rather defending the tenets of the Nicene Creed. What appears of particular importance in the passage under investigation is that, because Calvin adheres to this view of Christ's natures, he sees the (true) Church as the very real physical presence of Christ on earth, which his spiritual nature transcends.

---

91. Calvin, *Epistles of Paul*, 388.

92. Calvin, *Institutes* 4.27.1–34.

93. Calvin hammered out an agreement known as the *Consensus Tigurinus* (1549) with Bullinger, Zwingli's successor at Zurich, in order to minimize their differences over the Eucharist. Many Lutherans saw this as a move on Calvin's part further away from Lutheranism. Most notable was Tilemann Hesshusen, who published *De Praesentia Corporis Christi in Coena Domini, contra Sacramentarios* against Calvin. Calvin responded in kind with *Dilucida Explicatio Sanae Doctrinae de Vera Participatione Carnis et Sanguinis in Sacra Coena, ad Discutiendas Hashusii Nebulas*. See Steinmetz, *Calvin in Context*, 172–74; Calvin, *Theological Treatises*, 22:257–324.

In this way, Christians are compelled to rejoice at any goodness experienced by the body, because a Spiritual animating force unites those physical parts.

The next prominent section in which Calvin attends to the nature of the Church is the third chapter of the epistle. In Paul's prayer "that the word of the Lord may run" (3:1) Calvin sees the apostle concerned for the entire Church, because it demonstrates primarily concern for "the glory of Christ and the common welfare of the Church," rather than (exclusively) Paul's personal interests.[94] The desire has to do with the unhindered dissemination of the gospel, which is clarified by "even as also it is with you" (3:1). Therefore, the Church is characterised by "those who have already entered the kingdom" and who pray in such a way, with the larger desire that God may bring about its complete manifestation.[95]

Drawing a connection between the Lord as the ultimate source of Paul's commands and the apostle's confidence that the Thessalonians will do as he has commanded (3:4), Calvin makes a decidedly contextually-shaped observation. The verse "defines the limits to his demands as well as to their obedience—it should only be to the Lord. Any, therefore, who do not observe this restriction offer Paul's example for the purpose of fettering the Church and subjecting it to their laws to no purpose."[96] This is a markedly unveiled reference to the Catholic traditions. The "true" Church exhibits freedom from obedience to extraneously imposed (non-biblical) conditions, even should they come from an ecclesiastical authority. Though Paul likely did not *intend* this meaning, he created the *potential* for such a reading in a context where the location of the Lord's "voice" was debated.

On the "disorderly/idle" (3:6–10), Calvin perceives the apostle to be addressing a particular issue regarding idle members of the community "who do not have any honourable or useful occupation."[97] He sees these as individuals living for themselves, who forget their necessary loving service to their neighbour, and who fail to help others. Following Chrysostom, he argues that the Church must, as a command of Christ, sever fellowship with such "disorderly" Christians because they dishonour the body of Christ and "they are the taints and blots of religion."[98] The aim of exclusion, he clarifies, is to bring about repentance and their return to the community

---

94. Calvin, *Comm. 2 Thess* (CO 52:208).
95. Calvin, *Epistles of Paul*, 413.
96. Calvin, *Epistles of Paul*, 415.
97. Calvin, *Epistles of Paul*, 416.
98. Calvin, *Epistles of Paul*, 417.

(3:6, 14–15). He even cites the example of Simon Magus as not one cast into despair, but offered the opportunity to repent (Acts 8:22). Therefore, Simon's desire for self-advancement through purchasing the power of the Holy Spirit represents an example of a "disorderly" congregant.[99] He broadens the category to include more than just those who do not work. Nevertheless, Calvin turns the text on monks as a prime example of non-working "Christians," who make demands of sustenance on others.[100] This too fits under his perspective that the title "disorderly" applies to all who are self-focused.

In addition to bringing about repentance, Calvin sees the purpose of this excommunicative practice as preventative of tarnishing the Christian name and dishonoring God, as well as protecting the corruption of good people.[101] He unites the power to "bind and loose" (Matt 16:19) given by Christ with Paul's insistence on disciplinary exclusion (2 Thess 3:6–15). Because of this, damnation is assured if the offender fails to repent, but the Church must cautiously and gently administer it "lest we slide from discipline to butchery."[102]

In summary, Calvin's vision of the Church, as it relates to 2 Thessalonians, entails a physical "body" of believers connected on a foundational level and animated by the life-giving Spirit of God. Any good (and conversely any negative experience) endured by an individual or segment thereof affects the entire body, and therefore necessitates a response of gratitude toward the Source of the body. Those within the true Church have already entered the kingdom of God and earnestly pray for its complete manifestation. Until that day, they dwell under scripture as the sole voice of authority (or at least a particular reading of it), using it for daily guidance, including the administration of discipline.

Eschatology

Eschatology, quite fittingly, is the final theological influence on Calvin to receive consideration. Again, this topic overlaps a great deal with material

---

99. Calvin, *Institutes* 4.1.26. The association of Simon with 2 Thessalonians at a different location likely indicates the influence of reception history.

100. Calvin, *Institutes* 4.13.11. He draws this conclusion with relationship to 2 Thess 3:11.

101. Calvin, *Institutes* 4.12.5.

102. Calvin, *Institutes* 2:4.12.10

from 2 Thess 2, which we have reserved for the final section of this chapter, and therefore we avoid encroachment where possible. Generally speaking, neither Calvin nor Luther developed a coherent system of "the last things," and on specific doctrines such as the "intermediate state, resurrection, return of Christ, judgment, and the future kingdom of God" Calvin offered "no creative reformulation of the church's eschatology."[103] The Reformers' apparent reticence to develop a precise eschatology was due in part to a perceived misuse of the doctrine amongst Catholics and fanatics, albeit for different ends.[104] This hesitation with regard to eschatology likely accounts for Calvin's failing to produce a commentary on Revelation, despite offering commentaries on the remainder of the NT.

All of this does not mean, however, that Calvin's theology is devoid of an eschatological perspective. Despite his moderate eschatological position with regard to specific doctrines, Calvin's theology is thoroughly *eschatologically-oriented*. Three primary aspects, hierarchically arranged, shape this orientation: Christ, history, and hope. Calvin eagerly expects the return of Christ and the consummation of history, but this expectation is founded upon the reality of Christ's resurrection and the biblical assurance of his return. That reality enables him to live in the present with a mind toward the end, seeking actively to bring it about. This dominance of Christ in his gaze toward the eschaton leads Quistorp to assert that, for Calvin, "eschatology is Christology."[105]

It should be evident in the preceding description how history and hope fall into place under Christ in Calvin's "eschatology." With the former, "the advent of Christ, his death and resurrection, is for Calvin the eschatological turning point of world history. At that moment the renovation of the world . . . was completed in Jesus Christ. . . . Every subsequent event can have meaning only in relationship to that 'renovation of the world which took place at the advent of Christ.'"[106] Thus "the ascended Christ holds together

---

103. Holwerda, "Eschatology and History," 133.

104. Quistorp helpfully describes fanatical misuse for "apocalyptic purposes," whereas Holwerda's emphasis in this regard on Calvin's "basic anti-apocalyptic bias" we find less precise and necessitating nuance given our understanding of "apocalyptic" (Quistorp, *Calvin's Doctrine*, 11; Holwerda, "Eschatology and History," 148).

105. Quistorp, *Calvin's Doctrine*, 22, 192.

106. Holwerda, "Eschatology and History," 142. The latter portion of the quote is taken from Calvin's commentary on Gen 17:7 with reference to the Abrahamic covenant (Calvin, *Commentarius in Genesin*, 1:200).

the Advent and Return," governing all time and standing "at the center of Calvin's eschatological vision."[107]

In a way, Calvin's perspective reminds us of Haimo's understanding that all time following the redemption of the cross is eschatological. Calvin's unique contribution with regard to history and time, however, is in his establishing these concepts in everyday life and seeing dynamic movement in history toward something, namely the kingdom of God, as opposed to the static view of history held within the Church of his time.[108] Both the view of Christ and time/history are concretised in the *hope* of the believer. All three of these themes underlie his reading of 2 Thessalonians.

His eschatological perspective of Christ remains largely implicit until his comment on 2 Thess 2:3, in which he describes the world as already "under the rule of Christ."[109] This perspective assumes the reality of the resurrection, yet it allows for the seeming contradiction of this rule with perceived reality in light of the necessary judgment to come. Through this perspective (Calvin's vision of God as the righteous judge of the world, who inflicts vengeance on the unjust and glorifies his saints) Calvin asserts "the principle of faith"[110]—a principle that is inextricably linked to "hope" for the Reformer.[111] This faith entails both trust and assurance in God's plan for history. Expanding outward from the central platform of Christ, history, and hope, Calvin incorporates Christian suffering, contempt for the world, and Christian responsibility for ushering in the kingdom of God into his eschatology.

As Calvin sees it, suffering for one's faith breeds necessary "contempt" for the world and sets one's mind "on things beyond: the retribution of Christ"[112] so that "whatever annoyances we suffer foreshadow to us the life to come."[113] Rather than concentrate on the affliction suffered by the ungodly in the judgment, Calvin regards this as a distraction from the aim "that the godly should pass over this brief course of their earthly life

---

107. Holwerda, "Eschatology and History," 144.

108. Harbison, "History and Destiny," 395–97. Harbison credits Calvin with the modern perception of historical "progress."

109. Calvin, *Epistles of Paul*, 399.

110. Calvin, *Epistles of Paul*, 389.

111. For the regulatory function of hope in faith in Calvin, see Quistorp, *Calvin's Doctrine*, 16–22.

112. Calvin on 2 Thess 1:6–7 (Calvin, *Institutes* 3.9.5).

113. Calvin on 2 Thess 1:6–8 (Calvin, *Institutes* 3.25.10).

with eyes closed and their minds ever intent on the future manifestation of Christ's kingdom."[114]

Yet he ensures moderation against an overly-anticipatory eschatology by noting that Paul reminds his readers to think of the *eschaton* only with reverence and restraint (2:1)[115] and, following the apostle's emphasis (2:3), "that believers are to wage a protracted conflict before they gain the victory."[116] Only in this frame of mind are believers to "despise the world, put to death the flesh, and endure the Cross."[117]

Calvin owes a great deal to the formative work of Thomas à Kempis, *De imitatione Christi*, which dominated the devotional life of students in Paris during Calvin's period of matriculation there, for his denunciatory view of the world.[118] It would be a misconception, however, to describe Calvin's vision of Christian suffering and contempt for the world as an unmitigated reception of à Kempis's position. The latter proposes a very literal contempt for the world that leads to withdrawal and concentration on the interior life.

Alternatively, Calvin urges gratitude for earthly life, and "contempt for the world" has to do with the "rejection of what is *evil*, and a recognition that true life must be sought in Christ."[119] In Calvin's thought, then, "the world" functions as a foil to "the heavenly," though it does not rule out the presence of the heavenly in the world. Belief in the gospel, as Calvin would have it, transports the heart of the believer by means of hope into the heavenly presence of Christ so that they eagerly anticipate the day in which they fully participate in his glory; when their home and their location become one. This eschatological focus prevents them from fastening to "earthly pleasures,"[120] but it has necessary ramifications for life in the world, not a retreat from the world, as à Kempis would suggest.

---

114. Calvin on 2 Thess 1:10 (Calvin, *Epistles of Paul*, 393).

115. Calvin, *Epistles of Paul*, 396.

116. Thus he provides a sure guard against the "Chiliasts" (Calvin, *Epistles of Paul*, 398).

117. In this way Calvin summarizes "the patience of Christ" (3:5) (Calvin, *Epistles of Paul*, 416).

118. Torrance, *Hermeneutics of John Calvin*, 74; Holwerda, "Eschatology and History," 138–39. For the widespread dissemination of à Kempis, see Pelikan, *Christian Tradition*, 4:36–37.

119. Holwerda, "Eschatology and History," 139 (emphasis added).

120. Calvin, *Institutes* 2.10.3.

In Calvin's eschatology, Christians aid in bringing the world "under the rule of Christ" through the ongoing preaching of the word against the kingdom of Antichrist, which Calvin equates with the Lord Jesus slaying him "with the breath of his mouth" (2:8).[121] They also undergird this mission by continually praying "that the word of the Lord (i.e., preaching) may run" (3:1),[122] seeking to usher in the fullness of God's kingdom, so that their earthly and heavenly lives might be unified.

During the time of suspension between the ascension and second coming, Christians manifest their eschatological hope via ethical continuity with the heavenly kingdom. Thus, believers must persist in "love for God and in the hope of Christ's coming" (cf. 3:5) as a general principle for living in the world. In the specific situation of work and daily life, Calvin sees "disorderly" (3:6) behavior as a failure to consider "the purpose for which we were formed and not to order our lives with the end in view, for it is only when we live in accordance with the rule of God that our life is set in order."[123]

In many ways, this eschatological current is reminiscent of Chrysostom, though perhaps more full-bodied in the manner that Calvin employs it. Moreover, the beauty of Calvin's eschatological reading is its ability to unify the content of all three chapters of the epistle by means of a theological basis—a difficult task for some modern readers of 2 Thessalonians.[124]

The above discussion should render apparent that, though Calvin does not develop an eschatology proper, an eschatological perspective imbues his theological reading of 2 Thessalonians. Yet all this eschatology entails must be considered as intimately related with and subservient to his Christology.[125] One crucial difference between Calvin and Luther is that Calvin did not speak of the time of Christ's second advent. An emphasis on the Parousia, though not inherently negative, could lead to an apocalyptic enthusiasm that Calvin wanted to avoid. Instead, "the basic thrust

---

121. Calvin, *Epistles of Paul*, 405.

122. Calvin, *Epistles of Paul*, 413.

123. Calvin, *Epistles of Paul*, 416. "Calvin's eschatological vision is in essence a call for decision and obedient action here and now" (Holwerda, "Eschatology and History," 153).

124. Best, for example, can see 2 Thess 3 as only "loosely attached" to the material that precedes (Best, *Thessalonians*, 322). See also Marshall, *1 and 2 Thessalonians*, 212. Even Witherington has difficulty in connected 3:6ff with the rest of the letter, except to note that it is simply the beginning of a new section (Witherington III, *1 and 2 Thessalonians*, 245).

125. Quistorp, *Calvin's Doctrine*, 54; Placher, *Domestication of Transcendence*, 98–99.

of [Calvin's] eschatological teaching is not to produce calculation, but patience and hope."[126] A review of eschatology and 2 Thessalonians for any scholar would not be complete, however, without giving detailed attention to their reading of 2 Thess 2.

THE PAPACY AND THE ANTICHRIST

This section focuses on Calvin's interpretation of 2 Thess 2:1-12, drawing into the discussion the historical and theological influences on his reading without looking in extensive detail at the breadth of the latter as it relates to the rest of his work(s). Like his predecessors, Calvin believes Paul is offering an apocalyptic timeline, though he recognizes it as a symbolic-spiritual prophecy regarding the future, thereby situating himself in the Tyconian-Augustinian interpretive tradition with regard to 2 Thessalonians.

From the outset of the timeline, Calvin differentiates himself from his predecessors because he does not see Paul's words as an exclusive prediction of the future, but also as a reality that began immediately after the ascension of Christ. The Lord had to first establish his kingdom in order for individuals to begin their "rebellion" (3:3) against it.[127] He rejects the fall of the Roman Empire as "highly absurd"[128] for an explanation for "apostasy." Instead, he proposes that the term "apostasy" must mean a rebellion by "those who have previously enlisted in the service of Christ and His Gospel."[129] This may seem a reference to the papacy, but it is broader than that for Calvin both categorically and historically. In the *Institutes*, he clarifies that the apostasy first entails pastors forsaking God, which he sees already at work in Paul's warning against false teachers who have "wandered away" (1 Tim 1:6).[130]

From the foundation of Christ's kingdom, then, the apostasy has been in effect. Calvin adds to this apostasy all sects and heresies, including Islam, for he regards Mohammed as an apostate, who "turned his followers, the Turks, from Christ" and "tore away about half of the Church."[131] It is

126. Holwerda, "Eschatology and History," 149.

127. "Paul declares that when the world has been brought under the rule of Christ, *a defection will take place*" (Calvin, *Epistles of Paul*, 399).

128. "Magis frivolum" (Calvin, *Comm. 2 Thess* [CO 52:196]).

129. Calvin, *Epistles of Paul*, 399.

130. Calvin, *Institutes* 4.9.7.

131. Calvin, *Epistles of Paul*, 399-400. In his commentary on 1 John 2:18-19, Calvin

crucial for Calvin to establish this reading against the "Romanists" in order to justify the Reformation movement, yet he is battling both a static view of history, the prevalent view held within the Catholic Church regarding its ontological status, and a particular reading of the epistle by Bruno the Carthusian (d. 1101).

Bruno develops Ambrosiaster's interpretation into an emphasis that the apostasy entails "falling away" from the dual, intertwined, "Christian empires, both secular (such as kings), and spiritual (that is, the pope)."[132] The rebellion takes place primarily against the "spiritual empire," which he reads as a collective unfaithful movement as depicted in the first beast of Rev 13. Until the date of the apostasy, these unfaithful exist as a hidden body within the Church.[133]

In the centuries following Bruno, however, interpretation of 2 Thess 2:1-12 followed this reading of the spiritual revolt in part, but incorporated a crucial modifier: Antichrist would arise as the leader of the Church, a concept that was unimaginable for Bruno.[134] Calvin, therefore, must not only prove that his movement is not the apostasy, but also that his reading more faithfully represents the NT, particularly 2 Thessalonians, and he is able to do so by accessing the more recent interpretive tradition.

Like Bruno (as well as Augustine), Calvin immediately takes the "temple of God" as a reference to the Church without seriously considering the other possibility.[135] He even agrees that Paul's words function prophetically in describing a rebellion from the Church, though Calvin's perspective differs in that he describes Paul as anticipating the ongoing rebellion of the faithful. It is not a large group in a single movement. Antichrist is part of this rebellion, but with the specific function of battling the true Church within the physical Church.

---

describes the heretics Cerinthus, Basilides, Marcion, Valentinus, Ebion, and Arius as both part of the apostasy and the mystery of iniquity that precede the Antichrist proper. See Calvin, *Commentarius in Iohannis Apostoli epistolam* (CO 55:322-23). Here, Calvin also rejects a medieval tradition, disseminated especially through Innocent III, which equated Islam with Antichrist (McGinn, *Antichrist*, 150-52).

132. For this translation of Bruno, see Hughes, *Constructing Antichrist*, 197.

133. Hughes, *Constructing Antichrist*, 198-99.

134. Pelikan, *Christian Tradition*, 4:38. This can certainly be seen in Wycliffe and Hus, but is found even earlier in Frederick II Hohenstaufen (1194-1250), Peter Olivi (1248-98), and Ubertino of Casale (1259-1330). McGinn, *Antichrist*, 152-66.

135. In his opening sentence on 2 Thess 2:3, Calvin describes the entire passage as "a gloomy prediction concerning *the future dispersion of the Church*" (Calvin, *Epistles of Paul*, 398 [emphasis added]).

As the pre-Antichrist rebellion continues to unfold in history, Satan, meanwhile, lays a foundation upon which Antichrist might openly stand against the kingdom of Christ. Satan accomplishes this through the work of individuals who slowly build up the power of the papacy into the form that appears in Calvin's day. This rebellious work, preceding the outward manifestation of Antichrist, Calvin regards as the "mystery of iniquity" (2 Thess 2:7), yet he also considers all of those who aided in its development as belonging to the kingdom of Antichrist by pointing to those rebellious individuals already present in the days of John (1 John 2:18).[136] The secret work of Antichrist would begin at an early stage so that it could affect the practice of many and appear as the appropriate form of Church until Antichrist could confidently and finally assert his position.

In the meantime (i.e., for Paul and the early Church) a "restraint" (τό κατέχον; 2 Thess 2:6) restricts the open appearance of this Antichrist kingdom. Calvin argues that Paul means "the doctrine of *the Gospel* was to spread far and wide until almost the whole world had been convicted of obstinacy and wilful malice."[137] Two influences are likely at work in this exegetical decision: 1.) the neuter gender of κατέχον and εὐαγγέλιον, and; 2.) Chrysostom's introductory homily, in which he describes one of the primary signs to precede the second advent of Christ is the preaching of the gospel to all nations (Matt 24:14).

In terms of reception history, Calvin shifts Chrysostom's reading of gospel proclamation as a generic sign to a central location by understanding it as the nebulous referent, τό κατέχον, which must precede the arrival of Antichrist. His modification marks a break with the Church Father, for in advancing gospel proclamation as τό κατέχον, he rejects Chrysostom's position regarding the Roman Empire. Calvin offers a concession by noting that the eventual collapse of the Roman Empire would be an appropriate time for Antichrist to seize the opportunity, and is indeed what happened.[138] Thus, historical events and Paul's prophecy coincided, but

---

136. Calvin, *Epistles of Paul*, 404; *Institutes* 4.7.25. Augustine also shares this canonical reading. The difference in Calvin's work lays in his refusal to recognize Antichrist as an individual, which Augustine admits, but then offers a spiritual reading because of the passage's obscurity.

137. Calvin, *Epistles of Paul*, 402 (emphasis added).

138. Chrysostom, *In epist. ii ad Thess* 4 (PG 62:486–87). Calvin clearly regards this as an event that has already taken place: "There is not one of these things that was not later confirmed in actual experience" (Calvin, *Episltes of Paul*, 403). It is likely that Calvin followed the perspective found in *History from the Decline of the Roman Empire*, by Flavio

The Reformation

they were not the same. Of course, this view of the restraint accords with Calvin's perspective of divine sovereignty, in which "the grace of God was to be offered to all . . . by his Gospel, in order that men's impiety might be more fully attested. This, therefore, was the delay until the course of the Gospel was completed."[139] Through the revivifivation and modification of Chrysostom's work Calvin inaugurates a decidedly unique interpretation of τό κατέχον. In Calvin's paradigm and historical context, Chrysostom's interpretation does not adequately answer the questions that the Reformer poses to the text.

Berengar of Tours (d. 1088) saw "that which restrains" as the completion of a divinely ordained period, marked by when the "fullness of the Gentiles enters the faith."[140] But this is not necessarily the same as the proclamation of the gospel to all nations. The two scholars discover a similar solution to the enigmatic phrase from different angles. The older scholar considers the end that brings a conclusion to an era, while the Reformer

---

Biondo (published in 1483), which marked Rome's decline with the Visigoth invasion (410) of Rome. Both Machiavelli and, in a modified form, Melanchthon took up this viewpoint. See Little, "Calvin's Appreciation," 368. For Calvin, the turmoil in Europe initiated by the Visigoth invasion, then exacerbated by the Vandal invasion (455) distracted from the developments in the Roman See. The widespread strife in the Christian world generations later during the time of Gregory I (d. 604), however, resulted in the elevation of the Roman See for necessary spiritual stability in the midst of much uncertainty. Corruption, in many ways inadvertent, matured throughout these eras of upheaval, but it varied from pope to pope. For example, Calvin generally excludes Pope Gregory I (d. 604) from negative evaluation, though he is less friendly toward Leo I (d. 461). As "the last bishop of Rome," in Calvin's eyes, Gregory still denied the supremacy of the papacy as the universal patriarch in reaction to the claim by John of Constantinople for that title. Gregory went so far as to declare that it marked the nearness of Antichrist. See Calvin, *Institutes* 4.7, 4.17.49; He asserts more directly that the "purer doctrine flourished" during the first five hundred years of the Church (Calvin, *Institutes* 1.11.13). Taking all of this into consideration, it becomes apparent how Calvin can assert the coinciding of Chrysostom's view that the "falling away" of Rome with the appearance of Antichrist without accepting his interpretation.

139. Calvin, *Epistles of Paul*, 403. One must conclude from this that Calvin believes that the Gospel has been preached to every nation. Holwerda, "Eschatology and History," 150.

140. "Quo plenitudo gentium intrat ad fidem"—Berengar of Tours in Lombard, *In epist. ii ad Thess* (PG 192:318). Hughes reads this passage in Lombard's work as the fulfilment of the "great commission." The concept utilized by Berengar, however, is from Rom 11, not Matt 28:18-20. See Hughes, *Constructing Antichrist*, 232-33. Nevertheless, Calvin speaks of "de universali gentium vocatione" on the same verse (Calvin, *Comm. 2 Thess* [CO 52:200]).

sees the means as the grammatically linked emphasis.[141] After this restraint disappears,[142] Satan's substantial construction of a suitable foundation for the "lawless one," and the various sects and heresies have distracted attention, then Antichrist will appear. As noted above, Antichrist is better thought of as a kingdom composed of many individuals, yet Paul describes him as "a single individual, because it is a single reign, though there is a succession of individuals."[143] Calvin sets up an interpretation that allows one to read the papacy as Antichrist.

Following a historical trend, Calvin perceives Antichrist as in "diametrical opposition to Christ,"[144] taking his cue from 2 Thess 2:4 in the lawless one's counter claims to Christ. Later, Calvin draws the relationship between a biblical description of what belongs to God and the manner in which the pope claims them for himself. Among these powers Calvin lists the power of salvation (in terms of means and method), the implementation of ecclesiastical laws and doctrines,[145] and the creation of sacraments.[146] Following a traditional interpretation found in both Chrysostom and Haimo (against several modern commentators), Calvin agrees that Satan will perform "false miracles" (2 Thess 2:9–10) through Antichrist "by means of trickery"[147] and not with genuine miracles, and he points to this as further evidence that the papacy is Antichrist. This complies with Calvin's perception of Antichrist as diametrically opposed with Christ, yet the point is somewhat nebulous.

---

141. Through Bede's reading of Rev 20, Riddlebarger brings together the interpretive perspectives of Berengar, Calvin, and Nicholl (Riddlebarger, *Man of Sin*, 131–32).

142. He understands this from "And then" in the phrase "And then shall be revealed the lawless one" (2:8) (Calvin, *Epistles of Paul*, 404).

143. Calvin, *Epistles of Paul*, 400. He clarifies later that the singular case is due to the fact that it describes a single kingdom "which extends through many generations." In so doing, he is also able to resolve the tension between 2 Thess 2:3 and 1 John 2:18–19. See Calvin, *Epistles of Paul*, 404.

144. Calvin, *Epistles of Paul*, 400.

145. He clarifies this point in his commentary on 1 Tim 4:1–5. As examples of corrupt doctrines, Calvin offers the consumption of meat on certain days of the week and the prohibition of marriage for monks and priests, which Calvin sees as idolatrous because they redirect attention toward the practice and away from God. Calvin, *Commentarius in epistolam Pauli ad Timotheum i* (CO 52:292–98). See also his *Commentarius in Iacobi Apostoli epistolam* (CO 55:420) for the connection between "one lawgiver" (James 4:12) and declaring the Pope Antichrist.

146. Calvin, *Epistles of Paul*, 401; Calvin, *Institutes* 2:4.2.12; 4.7.24–25; 4.9.7.

147. Calvin, *Epistles of Paul*, 406.

He clarifies this the preface of the *Institutes*, in which he reveals that his opponents have demanded miracles of him to confirm the truth of his message. He argues that the Reformers' gospel does not diverge from the historical Church and that a "miracle" verifies nothing for even Satan exhibits himself as an angel of light (2 Cor 11:14). His opponents could then turn the miracle against him. So, Calvin addresses the apparent miracles offered by the Papists as evidence for the veracity of the Roman Church, highlighting particularly unspecified wonders wrought by the relics of saints. This only serves as fodder for Calvin's interpretation of 2 Thess 2:9–10 because he contends that draw people away from the worship of God, which coincides with the desires of Satan.[148]

Calvin recognizes that the duration of Antichrist's kingdom will be extensive and the true Church will suffer. Yet, quite distinct from the traditional interpretation, Calvin sees the destruction of Antichrist by means of "the breath of [Christ's] mouth" (2 Thess 2:8) as a reference to Christ's word (cf. Isa 11:4) as *the gospel*. For Calvin, this means that the destruction of Antichrist is not a single event at the end of history, but rather it is a gradual destruction brought about by the proclamation of Christ's truth by the elect. Thus Calvin undergirds the objective and legitimacy of the Reformation against the Catholic Church. The second advent of Christ receives only brief mention, but it marks the complete disappearance of Antichrist's kingdom.[149] Calvin situates the entire reading within his perspective of divine sovereignty, reading ὁ κατέχων as a future participle to indicate the God's role as one who delimits the temporal reign of Antichrist.[150]

Given the levels of corruption in the Church during Calvin's life, including even the papacy,[151] and the influence of Augustine's spiritual interpretation of 2 Thess 2:1–12, it is not entirely shocking that the reception of the text veered in this direction. Calvin's reading of this passage is a summit-dialogue of several authors. Taking traditions from Chrysostom—notably his reference to the essential precursor of the gospel going to all nations

---

148. Calvin, *Institutes*, 17.

149. Calvin, *Epistles of Paul*, 405.

150. Calvin, *Epistles of Paul*, 404.

151. Issues of licentiousness, simony, extravagance, and nepotism plagued the papacy in examples such as Boniface VIII (d. 1303) through the Avignon papacy, the Western Schism, and during the Reformation (e.g., Leo X). Catholic critics ranged from the author Dante to the theologian Erasmus. See González, *Story of Christianity*, 2:6–13. We might add to this the reassertion of the view by Cusa that councils had the right to correct an erring pope. Pelikan, *Christian Tradition*, 4:105–6.

and the acceptance of the apocalyptic timeline as a literal description of events—and the Tyconian-Augustine spiritual tradition in reading 2 Thess 2:1–12 as referring to the Church—Calvin blends the two systems so that the apocalyptic timeline becomes a *literal* description of events that will unfold within the Church. This new tradition rapidly became a dominant Protestant reading of 2 Thessalonians with ramifications extending even to certain streams of Protestantism today. Calvin's exegesis of 2 Thess 2:1–12 does not materialise in a vacuum. In addition to these patristic sources, he builds upon the work and insights of closer predecessors, most notably Luther.

On this passage, the Catholic scholars, Cajetan and Estius, follow the more literal-historical reading of Ambrosiaster and Jerome. Cajetan in particular adds little of interest to the discussion. Estius has the responsibility of reinforcing the traditional interpretation in the aftermath of the Reformation. Therefore, he recognizes the Roman Pontiff as the heir of and spiritual leader over the Roman Empire[152] and the "apostasy" (2:3) as a rebellion from this leadership. In so doing, he perfectly characterizes the Reformation as the apostasy and the "mystery of iniquity at work" (2:7), and thus on the wrong side of the eschatological battle.[153] It means as well that Antichrist, whom Estius believes to be an individual who will function as the "chief organ of the devil,"[154] has not yet arrived. He even rebukes the Reformers for labelling the papacy as Antichrist because, to him, it would mean that Peter the apostle was Antichrist.[155] He engages with Augustine's readings only occasionally and cursorily, regarding him as less concrete on the passage than other Fathers.

---

152. It becomes clear throughout his work, but particularly in his emphasis that the Roman Empire is "that which restrains" (2:6), that Estius has adopted the "two swords" perspective of the world propagated first by Pope Gelasius and demonstrated in Bruno the Carthusian's commentary on 2 Thessalonians. In this perspective, secular power lies with Christian kings and spiritual authority resides in the papacy. See Hughes, *Constructing Antichrist*, 197–200. His citation of Gelasius renders the above point stronger. See Estius, *In omnes D. Pauli*, 749.

153. Estius, *In omnes D. Pauli*, 747, 749.

154. "Erit igitur Antichristus homo, non diabolus, *sed diaboli praecipuum organum*" (Estius, *In omnes D. Pauli*, 747).

155. Estius, *In Omnes d. Pauli*, 749. Calvin responds to such a charge with the simple *practical* consideration that the papacy has strayed so far from Peter through lack of moral consistency that they cannot evidence their claims to be his heirs. See Calvin, *Institutes* 4.7.29.

THE REFORMATION

From the side of the Reformers, we see a continued utilisation of the spiritual interpretive tradition of 2 Thess 2:1-12. Zwingli offers a similar reading to Calvin, including a view of the "apostasy" (2:3) as false apostles and the papists,[156] the general declamation of the papacy as "Antichrist," and the perspective that this text is a prophecy by Paul concerning the future.[157] Yet his reading lacks the precision and sophistication of Calvin or Luther.

As noted above, it is with particular reference to this latter Reformer that Calvin's reading of 2 Thess 2:1-12 has been shaped. As could be expected, a large quantity of Luther's writings detail his perspective of the papacy, so we only offer a compressed vision.

Luther perceives the "mystery of lawlessness at work " (2:7) as the various heresies and sects that broke from the Church in the generations preceding the open revelation of Antichrist, and that will continue afterwards.[158] Antichrist cannot arrive, however, until the falling away (2:3) of the Roman Empire.[159] The divergence at this juncture is clear: Calvin reads the apostasy as religious rebellion, not political. The Reformers reunite, however, in Luther's conclusion that Antichrist is a plurality of individuals realised in a kingdom, namely the papacy.[160] Luther argues the titles "man of sin, the son of perdition" (2:3) fit the pope because he perpetuates sin through the insistence on works righteousness, the creation of practices he deems salvific while denying biblical practices, the misuse of the mass, his emphasis on the higher spirituality of monastics, and particularly in the permissive attitude toward sin in the offering of indulgences.[161] Above all

---

156. Zwingli as well perceives the true Church as in tact within the papal church, for he remarks that the phrase "apostasy" (*defectio*) is a synecdoche, for not all of the Church will fall away. See Zwingli, "In ii. epist. ad Thess," 241.

157. Zwingli, "In ii. epist. ad Thess," 241-44.

158. Luther, *Lectures on 1 John* (LW 30:253, 288); *This is my Body* (LW 37:16).

159. Luther, *Lectures on Zechariah* (LW 20:192). Luther shared the perspective that the Church can be divided into historical periods with reference to levels of corruption. Following on the example given above, though Luther speaks negatively of the instruction of purgatory by Gregory I, he still speaks of him as "a holy man" (Luther, *Misuse of the Mass* [LW 36:192]); though elsewhere he speaks less positively of the same man (Luther, *Lectures on Genesis* [LW 7:296-97]). The open eruption of corruption in the papacy is exemplified for Luther in the decretals of Gregory IX (d. 1241). See Luther, *Misuse of the Mass* (LW 36:138).

160. The pope is "the true, genuine, final Antichrist" (Luther, *Misuse of the Mass* [LW 36:219]).

161. See Luther, *Genesis* (LW 3:326; 7:344; 8:185); *Lectures on Galatians* (LW 26:335; 27:110); *Defense and Explanation* (LW 32:92); *Babylonian Captivity* (LW 36:72); *Misuse*

of this, Luther adds that it is not just the individual who is characterised by sin, but his entire "government."[162]

The implementation of indulgences leads into the manner in which the pope, as Antichrist, exalts himself above God (2:4), for he presumes to issue binding commands, which is the prerogative of God alone. Because the pope implements extraneous laws as binding, presumes to pronounce salvation, and takes on divine titles, he asserts himself above God, though Luther is careful to note that this is only in word and worship, yet not above his majesty, which would be impossible.[163] The pope asserts himself in this way in the Church—that is, "the temple of God" (2:4). In this realisation, Luther is careful to note that the true Church still exists within the one that Antichrist rules and that only spiritual, not physical separation can be attained in this age. It is for this reason of continued interconnection that Luther cautions the Anabaptists for rejecting everything associated with the papacy.[164] He expands this latter point with the Anabaptists by noting that, if the temple of God has still existed under and in spite of the papacy, then true baptism must have occurred during it. Since infant baptism was the dominant form of baptism, therefore, Luther marshals this in his list of

---

of the Mass (LW 36:151); Concerning the Ministry (LW 40:16). He goes so far as to assert that if it were for the insistence on clerical celibacy alone, the pope would be "the man of sin" (Luther, Answer to the Hyperchristian Book [LW 39:212]). Luther offers his most detailed explanation of why the pope is "the man of sin" in Luther, Answer to the Hyperchristian Book (LW 39:201–202). He even expands the terminology to "men of sin" so that he can include the "papists" in the condemnation. See Luther, Keys (LW 40:353).

162. Luther, Why the Books were Burned (LW 31:392).

163. Luther, Lectures on the Psalms (LW 13:190–91); Lectures on Isaiah (LW 16:109); Sermons on St. John (LW 22:470). He adds that anyone who practices a self-invented holiness (e.g., clerics and monks) exalts his/herself above God. See Luther, Zechariah (LW 20:263–64); Sermon on the Mount (LW 21:63); Galatians (LW 26:180, 257–59, 407–8); Lectures on 1 Timothy (LW 28:377); Defense and Explanation (LW 32:46, 66); Bondage of the Will (LW 33:139); Alleged Imperial Edict (LW 33:88–89; 34:67); Private Mass and the Consecration (LW 38:190); Keys (LW 40:349); Against the Heavenly Prophets (LW 40:129–30).

164. Luther, Against Latomus (LW 32:139); Private Mass (LW 38:210–11); Pelikan, Christian Tradition, 4:172–75. Luther notes that though the pope is stationed within the Church, technically he rules a synagogue. The logic behind this statement is that the pope offers a law of works for salvation, which characterizes Luther's view of Judaism (Luther, Lectures on Philemon [LW 29:102]). He largely assumes that "the temple of God" refers to the Church, but he offers his clearest definition of the "temple" as "Christendom" and openly rejects the notion that it intimates a building of "stones" (i.e., the Jerusalem temple) (Luther, Concerning Rebaptism [LW 40:232]).

arguments in favour of infant baptism.[165] In this way, Luther is able to put into play a particular interpretation of the passage in a different theological context with doctrinal ramifications.

The "strong delusion" (2:11) coincides with the decretals, doctrines, and requirements of the pope obeyed by the masses, but it extends even further to include any unreflective obedience to a command as salvific. Many of these "errors" entered long ago, as in Gregory's introduction of purgatory, but were overlooked as minor at the time, which was the insidious intention of Satan.[166] In Luther's present, they had amassed in a large volume and people followed them because they had been established in generations prior. The "strong delusion" is well deserved, in Luther's eyes, as individuals are responsible to engage with their traditions.[167] Those who adhere to these errors await their destruction by "the breath of [Christ's] mouth" (2:8).

Like Calvin, Luther sees this happening presently, beginning with Hus, in the proclamation of the Gospel against the papacy.[168] Different from Calvin, however, Luther includes strong statements about the second-advent of Christ as crucial to concluding this process of destruction.[169] Additionally, Luther establishes connections between 2 Thessalonians and Revelation that Calvin (and Haimo), as largely anti-apocalyptic, avoids.[170]

In many ways, therefore, Calvin builds upon Luther, though he provides a more precise and unified interpretation of 2 Thess 2:3–12. The advantage and distinction that Luther brings to this reading of the papal

---

165. Luther, *Rebaptism* (LW 40:257).

166. Luther, *Genesis* (LW 7:297); *Misuse of the Mass* (LW 36:192).

167. Luther's list of "delusions" is extensive and includes, but is not limited to, numerous teachings of the papacy (e.g., indulgences, the mass as sacrifice, the elevation of monasticism, purgatory, etc.) (Luther, *Genesis* [LW 2:354, 8:21]; *John* [LW 22:58, 24:268–69]; *Explanations of the Ninety-Five Theses* [LW 31:174–75, 205–6]; *This is my Body* [LW 37:142–43]); Islam in "Greece" (Luther, *Genesis* [LW 5:71]); pride (or as the result of pride) (Luther, *Genesis* [LW 4:127]; *First Psalm Lectures* [LW 10:462, 11:65]; *Psalms* [LW 14:246]; *John* [LW 22:137, 385]); and "peaceful preaching" rather than confrontation with the gospel (Luther, *Concerning the Answer of the Goat* [LW 39:133–34]).

168. Luther, *Genesis* (LW 8:226); *Concerning the Ministry* (LW 40:32). Unfortunately, this reveals that what Holwerda regards as the "most distinctive element in Calvin's perspective" has an interpretive precedent (Holwerda, "Eschatology and History," 151).

169. Luther, *Psalms* (LW 13:258).

170. Luther, *Prefaces to the New Testament* (LW 35:407).

Antichrist is to remove "the legendary historical accretions to the scriptural picture of Antichrist" amassed during the medieval period.[171]

Though Calvin exposits on well-trod ground by advocating a papal Antichrist,[172] he offers a number of keen insights to tighten up the vision relating to Antichrist in 2 Thess 2:3–12. His methodical reading of the letter reveals clearer parallels within the epistle and forces him to engage with difficult terminology, such as τό κατέχον and ὁ κατέχων, which Luther does not appear to address. For Calvin, the "falling away" (2:3) finds clearer explication in the NT (e.g., 1 Tim 1:6), rather than the OT (e.g., Luther's reading of Zech 2:8), and it describes a rebellion against God from within the Church.[173] He connects this with "the mystery of iniquity at work" (2 Thess 2:7), casting his gaze at historical heresies.

His most unique contributions, however, may be in reading τό κατέχον as a reference to the proclamation of the gospel and in blending the literal and spiritual patristic readings of 2 Thess 2:1–12. Calvin's interpretation has the ongoing potential to instil a healthy caution toward church leaders, regardless of their denominational leanings. Moreover, Calvin reveals that the power of Antichrist's kingdom, found within the Church, may only be overcome with the ongoing proclamation of the gospel. Potentially abstract theological concepts are grounded in accessible, daily praxis.

The obvious weakness of Calvin's interpretation and the overall framework within which he operates is his particular aversion to a dimension of apocalyptic eschatology, which results in a hesitancy to discuss the advent of Christ. As in Haimo's day, apocalyptic fervour surged during this new period of upheaval, admittedly from distinct stimuli. This reluctance does not, however, prevent Calvin from situating Christ at the centre of his theology.

---

171. McGinn, *Antichrist*, 207.

172. McGinn, *Antichrist*, 173–208. Luther and Calvin both carry forward the tradition of the papal Antichrist traced particularly (perhaps erroneously) to Grosseteste through Wyclif and Hus, though the tradition might be traced to earlier than 1,000 CE. See McGinn, *Antichrist*, 143–72. On Grosseteste, see McEvoy, *Robert Grosseteste*. Still, the answer to the question regarding the papacy and Antichrist is more readily received and sharply delimited during the Reformation.

173. Luther may be vaguely alluding to this idea when he describes the church as "being abandoned in its latest devastation by the Turk or Antichrist," but the reference is too nebulous to be certain (Luther, *Psalms* [LW 11:100]).

CONCLUSION

Though Calvin tends in his commentaries toward a singular, authorial meaning, much like his modern counterparts, his interpretation differs and is advantageous in at least two ways. First, he offers a distinctively "Calvinist" reading of 2 Thessalonians, both in terms of methodology and in conclusions. This entails a perspective that is contoured by a deep-seated pastoral concern for the average Christian, an eschatological understanding that demands a particular practical-ethical way of life,[174] and an all-encompassing grasp of God's sovereignty. All of these elements mature from Calvin's Christological centre, which functions as the governing concept in his theology and exegesis.

Second, though Calvin pursues Paul's "intention" and a singular meaning in the commentary, he lacks the same restrictions in the *Institutes*. In addition to the sections above, we might offer a brief example in his various emphases on the phrase "sanctification by the Spirit and belief in the truth" (2:13). Within his theological outlook, Calvin is variously able to assert that this phrase reveals Christ cannot be known apart from the sanctification of the Holy Spirit;[175] that the Spirit is qualified by the term "sanctification" because he builds up Christians presently, but is also the source of heavenly life;[176] that faith is the principal work of the Spirit and has no other source;[177] and that the "true" Church is delineated by the presence of the Holy Spirit.[178]

In terms of reception history, Calvin skilfully revives and modifies the Tyconian-Augustinian interpretation of 2 Thess 2:3–12. Because of this preservation, commentators must continue to engage the potential that "the temple of God" (2:4) can mean "the Church," as well as the distinctively Calvinist suggestion that τό κατέχον is the "proclamation of the gospel." He stands as an "epochal" interpreter of 2 Thessalonians for these above reasons, as well as the reincorporation of a pastoral perspective and the overt development of his own theological framework for understanding and guiding his exegesis. He is a prime example of both a reader shaped by

---

174. Hall describes these first two aspects as Calvin's concern for "edification and instruction," and he sees the source for it in the influence of biblical humanism (Hall, "Calvin and Biblical Humanism," 66).

175. Calvin, *Institutes* 3.2.8.

176. Calvin, *Institutes* 3.1.2.

177. Calvin, *Institutes* 3.1.4.

178. Calvin, *Institutes* 4.1.7.

particular exegetical impulses and one who provokes both past and present horizons of expectation.

5

Conclusion
Receiving 2 Thessalonians

"Antichrist"—an odd word for concluding a book aimed at participatory knowledge in God and deploying *Rezeptionsästhetik* as a "manuductive"[1] means for ordering the will to this self-same God. Yet, Antichrist plays such a critical role in the reception history of 2 Thessalonians, shaped especially by a canonical reading of 2 Thessalonians 2, 1 John 2–4, Revelation, and a long history of interpretation.

For John Chrysostom, Antichrist is a rhetorical foil to Jesus Christ and his apostle, Paul. By causing his readers to inhabit his canonically shaped virtue and vice reading of 2 Thessalonians, John elevates this epistle above the informational, eschatological-timeline approach to the book that characterizes much of its history.

Haimo of Auxerre follows John to an extent insofar as he reads in Antichrist a call to watchfulness against heresy. That is to say, Haimo uses the Antichrist to read 2 Thessalonians as an invective against heresy at large, with simony and double-predestination featuring from his context.

Calvin's vision is a bit more kaleidoscopic, witnessing various theological bursts throughout the epistle aimed at directing the reader to God. He attends to the Man of Lawlessness (i.e., Antichrist) as he appears within the letter, and not as its singular guiding principle. At his juncture in the

---

1. Candler, *Theology, Rhetoric, Manuduction*, 5.

reception history of 2 Thessalonians, Calvin is biblically and diachronically primed to see the papacy as a visible instantiation of Antichrist.

As epochal moments in the history of 2 Thessalonians, these interpreters' influence was/is due to the convergence of multiple factors: practical implications, fresh perspectives, influential personalities (in the cases of John Chrysostom and John Calvin), bringing together authoritative voices with unique contributions (Haimo), accessibility, contextual awareness, denominational allegiances, and any number of other reasons. But, above all, these readings have a historically high aesthetic register brought about through a balance of faithfulness to the content and genre of 2 Thessalonians and engagement with their own contexts, without venturing off into the fantastical that has led many other receptions to fall by the wayside of history.

At the same time, the *Rezeptionsästhetik* of 2 Thessalonians cannot be simply be reduced to a narrative about Antichrist or dated interpretations of bygone eras, nor should the *aesthetic* dimension of this method be simplified to chronological or synchronic comparisons. *Aesthetics* gauge the exegetical instances against the horizon of the original work, contemporary readings, modern interpretations, and the horizon of the Beautiful (and Infinite), disclosed historically in the form of God the Son. Furthermore, the *Rezeptions-* dimension and the *-ästhetik* dimension must remain together in order to avoid a return to the segregation of interpretation and theology that characterized scholarship for much of the eighteenth to the twentieth centuries. Let us look again at each of our historical interpreters to help bear out these receptive-aesthetic points.

John Chrysostom's overriding aim is the ordering of the desires and the will by cultivating virtue according to a vision of human nature. This hearkens back to Plato and Aristotle, but is refined and rendered in a biblical and Christological key (i.e., the image of God revealed in Jesus Christ), with metaphysical grounds bearing up courage, temperance, justice, and prudence alongside Christian virtues. Paul has discovered how to be(come) truly human through the imitation Christ, the true human. Therefore, follow Paul by doing what he says and minding how he says it.

For Haimo, though his reading attends in part to the speculative with regard to Antichrist, his larger objective is more Pauline insofar as the goal of the discussion is to orient the reader towards the Truth. Identification with Antichrist is not only an outward, confessional, and future action, but also a doctrinal stance permanently present in history. Adopting or

CONCLUSION

fabricating heresies situates one in the heretic-continuum inaugurated by Simon Magus and consummated in the arrival of Antichrist. Such acts are repeated denials of how God has revealed himself in Jesus Christ, and therefore they are acts of ontological violence in denying the Real. Paul speaks forcefully in the Carolingian context.

More so than Luther, Calvin is the fruition of medieval humanism for magisterial Protestantism: attention to original languages, cautious appropriation of the Church Fathers, and his emphasis on the practical import of reading the Bible. Calvin correlates biblical reading and practice for his audience—Jauss's emphasis on how texts must enter one's horizon of expectation and affect their social behavior.[2] The age of doctrines as abstractions without practical import for every Christian has disappeared. More importantly, Calvin marks a shift to text-centeredness (i.e., the written word) and away from receptions in art, architecture, and the Mass. His contextual reading foregrounds the reality of the threat of the corruption of the Church from within the community of believers. It is a clarion call to vigilant watchfulness in the Christian community and self-reflection, because those who affirm the faith, yet deny Christ with their actions belong to the historical body of the Antichrist.

In keeping with the program of *Rezeptionsästhetik*, Calvin's reading opens up questions for future generations. In particular, modern may readers continue to ask, "Is the pope still Antichrist?" especially in light of the end of Medici influence and papal political power, the Second Vatican Council, and the legacies of the popes particularly from the second half of the twentieth and early twenty-first centuries. This question has led some Protestant denominations even to remove this Reformation claim from the Westminster Confession of Faith.

What else has all of this to do with beauty and theological aesthetics? The *provisional* beauty of these readings subsists in the delight of understanding these temporally distant texts. Yet their meanings persist forever, insofar as they are "fitting"[3] to Divine Beauty, and they disclose their fullness as "beautiful" insofar as they participate in this locus of Beauty, to which we have access through the revelation of God the Son, the true form of Beauty. Furthermore, what reception history shows is, if these readings are faithful (i.e., *beautiful*), perhaps they are not separable as "traditions." Rather, they are *true* participations in scripture and, ultimately, deeper

---

2. Jauss, *Toward an Aesthetic*, 39.
3. On "fittingness" and aesthetics, see King, *Beauty of the Lord*, 9–17.

participations in the Triune God. They furnish the way of salvation (they do not contain it), by means of aiding in the ordering of the soul to God to bring about participatory knowledge, which is eternal life (John 17:3).

A larger goal of this project has been to suggest that the historical positivism that characterizes much of biblical studies is appropriate to some degree—Jesus lived and died; Paul composed foundational letters of the NT; words, in their original languages and conceptual systems, have a semantic range that delimits their interpretation; rhetorical arrangement and lexical selection can highlight the *intentions* of individual authors; it even accounts for the historicality of Christian belief. At the same time, this positivism lacks an ontological fullness to explain the claims of 2 Thessalonians by artificially and peremptorily marking off the boundaries of immanence and transcendence, or history and theology.[4] It can, for example, assert that Paul and John Calvin likely believed in God, but not that the God they believe in is real or the true God. This is only exacerbated by an anemic construal of "truth" as "fact" rather than as its identity with "being" and what that necessitates theologically and metaphysically.

Admittedly, "truth" and "being" may lie outside of the purview of history as a "science." Yet, it must assume first principles of being in order to work "meaningfully." It is for reasons like this that a theological reception aesthetics is better situated as a "method" than "pure" history. Jauss disrupts the essentially pragmatic approach to history by suggesting art history deals with perennial questions so long as readers continue to read a given text.[5] It follows that the meaning of a work, such as 2 Thessalonians, unfolds with time. This approach is easily baptized within an eschatological—interpretation in relation to the Christ-event and the consummation of history—and, more generally, a theological framework—meaning gauged in relation to the Real and proceeding from the infinite horizon of God.[6] Furthermore, in addition to (or perhaps "because of") a fuller sense of history and its theological coordination, this method may function as a means of cultivating desire for the truly beautiful through "constant exposure to countless instances of its advent."[7]

Receiving 2 Thessalonians ought entail a multi-faceted mindfulness of these various horizons: historical context, later interpretations, the reader's

4. Hart, *Beauty of the Infinite*, 13.
5. Jauss, *Toward an Aesthetic*, 46–75.
6. Hart, *Beauty of the Infinite*, 19.
7. Hart, *Beauty of the Infinite*, 18.

Conclusion

present, and the Infinite. As the historical dialogue with the text continues, old questions will refine our understanding of the epistle, all the while helping to generate new questions in the onward march of time. The program of theological reception aesthetics illuminates the "objective" beauty of 2 Thessalonians in the twilight of a relativistic age.

Bibliography

Adam, A. K. M. "Poaching on Zion: Biblical Theology as Signifying Practice." In *Reading Scripture with the Church: Toward a Hermeneutic for Theological Interpretation*, edited by A. K. M. Adam, et al., 17–34. Grand Rapids: Baker, 2006.

Ælfric of Eynsham. *Aelfric's Catholic Homilies: Introduction, Commentary, and Glossary*. Edited by Malcolm Godden. Oxford: Oxford University Press, 2000.

Alighieri, Dante. *Inferno: The Divine Comedy*. Translated by Allen Mandellbaum. New York: Bantam Dell, 1982.

Altaner, Berthold. "Augustinus und Johannes Chrysostomus." *ZNW* 44.1 (1953) 76–84.

Anderson, Gary A. "Ezekiel 28, the Fall of Satan, and the Adam Books." In *Literature on Adam and Eve: Collected Essays*, edited by Gary A. Anderson, et al., 133–48. Leiden: Brill, 2000.

The Apostolic Fathers. Translated by Bart D. Ehrman. Cambridge: Harvard University Press, 2003.

Augustine. *Against Julian*. Translated by Matthew A. Schumacher. Vol. 35 of FC. Washington, DC: Catholic University of America Press, 1957.

———. *Arianism and Other Heresies*. Edited by John E. Rotelle Translated by Roland J. Teske. Vol. 1.18 of *The Works of Saint Augustine: A Translation for the Twenty-First Century*. Hyde Park: New City, 1995.

———. *Confessions*. Translated by Henry Chadwick. Oxford: Oxford University Press, 2008.

———. *Enchiridion on Faith, Hope and Love*. Translated by Thomas S. Hibbs. Washington, DC: Regnery Gateway, 1996.

Backus, Irena. *Reformation Readings of the Apocalypse: Geneva, Zurich, and Wittenberg*. Oxford: Oxford University Press, 2000.

Barré, Henri. *Les homéliaires carolingiens de l'école d'Auxerre: authenticité, inventaire, tableaux comparatifs, initia*. Studi e Testi. Città del Vaticano: Biblioteca Apostolica Vaticana, 1962.

Barth, Karl. *The Theology of John Calvin*. Translated by Geoffrey W. Bromiley. Grand Rapids: Eerdmans, 1995.

Basil of Caesarea. *The Letters*. Translated by Roy J. Deferrari. 4 vols. LCL. London: William Heinemann, 1928.

Baum, Armin D. *Pseudepigraphie und literarische Fälschung im frühen Christentum: mit ausgewählten Quellentexten samt deutscher Übersetzung*. WUNT 2:138. Tübingen: Mohr Siebeck, 2001.

BIBLIOGRAPHY

Bavinck, Herman. "Of Beauty and Aesthetics." In *Essays on Religion, Science, and Society*, edited by John Bolt, 245-60. Translated by Harry Boonstra and Gerrit Sheeres. Grand Rapids: Baker, 2008.

Bede. *Excerpts from the Works of Saint Augustine on the Letters of the Blessed Apostle Paul.* Translated by David Hurst. Kalamazoo: Cistercian, 1999.

Beker, J. Christiaan. *Paul the Apostle*. Philadelphia: Fortress, 1980.

Bell, Richard H. *Deliver Us from Evil: Interpreting the Redemption from the Power of Satan in New Testament Theology.* Tübingen: Mohr Siebeck, 2007.

Best, Ernest. *A Commentary on the First and Second Epistles to the Thessalonians.* Edited by Henry Chadwick. Black's New Testament Commentaries. London: Adam & Charles Black, 1972.

Bockmuehl, Markus. "A Commentator's Approach to the 'Effective History' of Philippians." *JSNT* 18.69 (1995) 57-88.

Bonaventure. *Opera Omnia*. Paris: Ludovicus Vivès, 1865.

Bornemann, Wilhelm. *Die Thessalonicherbriefe*. Edited by H. A. W. Meyer. Kritisch-exegetischer Kommentar über das Neue Testament. Göttingen: Vandenhoeck & Ruprecht, 1894.

Boucaud, Pierre. "Claude de Turin et Haymon d'Auxerre." *Études d'exégèse carolingienne Autour d'Haymon d'Auxerre.* Edited by Sumi Shimahara. Collection Haut Moyen Âge 4. Turnhout: Brepols, 2007.

Bousset, Wilhelm. *The Antichrist Legend: A Chapter in Christian and Jewish Folklore.* Translated by A. H. Keane. Atlanta: Scholars, 1999.

Brandes, Wolfram. "Anastasios ὁ Δίκρος: Endzeiterwartung und Kaiserkritik." *ByzZ* 90.1 (1997) 24-63.

Brändle, Rudolf. *Johannes Chrysostomus*. Stuttgart: Kohlhammer, 1999.

———. "The Sweetest Passage: Matthew 25:31-46 and Assistance to the Poor in the Homilies of John Chrysostom." In *Wealth and Poverty in Early Church and Society*, edited by Susan R. Holman, 127-39. Grand Rapids: Baker Academic, 2008.

Breck, John. *Scripture in Tradition: The Bible and its Interpretation in the Orthodox Church.* Crestwood: St. Vladimir's Seminary Press, 2001.

Bright, Pamela. *The Book of Rules of Tyconius: Its Purpose and Inner Logic.* Notre Dame: University of Notre Dame Press, 2009.

Burgess, Richard W. *Studies in Eusebian and Post-Eusebian Chronology*. Stuttgart: Franz Steiner, 1999.

Burkitt, F. Crawford. *The Book of Rules of Tyconius*. Cambridge: Cambridge University Press, 1894.

Cajetan, Thomas. *Epistolae Pauli et aliorum apostolorum ad graecam veritatem castigatae.* Paris: Apud Iod. Badium Ascensium & Ioan. Paruum, & Ioannem Roigny, 1531.

Calvin, John. *Calvin: Theological Treatises*. Translated by J. K. S. Reid. Vol. 22 of *The Library of Christian Classics*. London: SCM, 1954.

———. *Commentaires de Jehan Calvin sur le Nouveau Testament: sur les Epistres de S. Paul aux Philippiens, Colossiens, Thessaloniciens, à Timothée, Tite, Philémon et aux Hébrieux, et sur les Epistres Canoniques de S. Pierre, S. Jehan, S. Jaques et S. Jude, autrement Appelées catholiques.* Paris: Librairie de Ch. Meyrueis et Compagnie, 1855.

———. *Commentarius in Genesin*. Edited by Ernst Wilhelm Hengstenberg. Vol. 1. Berlin: Gustavum Bethge, 1838.

———. *Commentaries on the Book of the Prophet Daniel*. Translated by Thomas Myers. Vol. 1. Edinburgh: Calvin Translation Society, 1852.

Bibliography

———. *Concerning the Eternal Predestination of God*. Translated by J. K. S. Reid. London: James Clarke, 1961.

———. *The Epistles of Paul the Apostle to the Romans and to the Thessalonians*. Edited by David W. Torrance and Thomas F. Torrance. London: Oliver and Boyd, 1961.

———. *Institutes of the Christian Religion*. Edited by John T. McNeill Translated by Ford Lewis Battles. Vol. 1 of *Library of Christian Classics*. Philadelphia: Westminster, 1960.

———. *Institutes of the Christian Religion*. Edited by John T. McNeill Translated by Ford Lewis Battles. Vol. 2 of *Library of Christian Classics*. Philadelphia: Westminster, 1960.

———. *Iohannis Calvini in omnes Pauli apostoli epistolas: epistolas ad Ephesios, Philippenses, Colossenses, Thessalonicenses, Timotheum, Titum, Philemonem, et Hebraeos Complectens*. Edited by August Tholuck. Vol. 2. Halis Saxonum: Librariae Gebaueriae, 1831.

———. *Ioannis Calvini opera quae supersunt omnia*. Edited by G. Baum, E. Cunitz, and E. Reuss. 59 vols. Corpus Reformatorum 29–87. Brunswick: Schwetschke, 1863–1900.

Candler, Peter. *Theology, Rhetoric, Manuduction, or Reading Scripture Together on the Path to God*. Radical Traditions. Grand Rapids: Eerdmans, 2006.

Cartwright, Steven R. "Thietland's Commentary on 2 Thessalonians: Digressions on the Antichrist and the End of the Millennium." In *The Apocalyptic Year 1000: Religious Expectation and Social Change, 950–1050*, edited by Richard Landes, et al., 93–108. Oxford: Oxford University Press, 2003.

Casiday, A. M. *Evagrius Ponticus*. Early Church Fathers. London: Routledge, 2006.

Charlesworth, James H., ed. *The Old Testament Pseudepigrapha*. 2 Vols. London: Doubleday, 1983.

———. *The Old Testament Pseudepigrapha and the New Testament*. SNTSMS 54. Cambridge: Cambridge University Press, 1985.

Chase, Frederic. *Chrysostom, a Study in the History of Biblical Interpretation*. Cambridge: Deighton, Bell, and Co., 1887.

Chrysostom, John. *On Repentance and Almsgiving*. Translated by Gus George Christo. Vol. 96 of *The Fathers of the Church*. Washington, DC: Catholic University of America Press, 1998.

Clarke, W. K. Lowther, ed. *The Ascetic Works of Saint Basil*. Translated by W. K. Lowther Clarke. London: Society for Promoting Christian Knowledge, 1925.

Colish, Marcia L. *Medieval Foundations of the Western Intellectual Tradition*. Edited by Robert Baldock. London: Yale University Press, 1997.

———. *Peter Lombard*. Vols. 1–2 of *Brill's Studies in Intellectual History*. Edited by A. J. Vanderjagt. Leiden: Brill, 1994.

Contreni, John J. "'By Lions, Bishops Are Meant; by Wolves, Priests': History, Exegesis, and the Carolingian Church in Haimo of Auxere's Commentary on Ezechiel." *Francia* 29.1 (2002) 29–56.

———. "Haimo of Auxerre, Abbot of Sasceium (Cessy-Les-Bois), and a New Sermon on 1 John v, 4–10." *RBén* 85 (1975) 303–20.

———. "Haimo of Auxerre's Commentary on Ezechiel." In *L'École carolingienne d'Auxerre: de Murethach à Rémi, 830–908*, edited by Dominique Iogna-Prat, et al., 229–42. L'histoire de l'actualité. Paris: Beauchesne, 1991.

Cooper, Kate. "An(n)ianus of Celeda and the Latin Readers of John Chrysostom." StPatr 27 (1993) 249–55.

Corrigan, Kevin. *Evagrius and Basil*. Farnham: Ashgate, 2009.

Bibliography

Cottret, Bernard. *Calvin: A Biography.* Translated by M. Wallace McDonald. Edinburgh: T. & T. Clark, 2000.

Cramer, J. A., ed. *Catenae graecorum patrum in Novum Testamentum.* 8 vols. Oxford: E Typographeo Academico, 1838-44.

Dowey, Edward A. *The Knowledge of God in Calvin's Theology.* Grand Rapids: Eerdmans, 1994.

Dressler, Hermigild, ed. *The Fathers of the Church.* 127 vols. Washington, DC: Catholic University of America Press, 1947.

Dudden, F. Homes. *Gregory the Great: His Place in History and Thought.* London: Longmans, Green, and Co., 1905.

Eldridge, Michael D. *Dying Adam with his Multiethnic Family.* SVTP. Leiden: Brill, 2001.

Elliott, Mark W. *The Heart of Biblical Theology: Providence Experienced.* Abingdon: Ashgate, 2012.

———. *Providence Perceived: Divine Action from a Human Point of View.* Arbeiten zur Kirchengeschichte. Berlin: De Gruyter, 2015.

Erasmus, Desiderius, ed. *Divi Chrysostomi Archepiscopi Constantinopolitani opera, quatenusin hunc diem latio Donate noscuntur, omnia.* Lutetiae Parisiorum: Apud Claudium Chevallonium, 1536.

Estius, Gulielmus. *In omnes d. Pauli epistolas item in catholicas commentarii.* Edited by Joannes Holzammer. Vol. 3. Moguntiae: Sumptibus Francisci Kirchhemii, 1859.

———. *In omnes d. Pauli & reliquas apostolorum epistolas.* Edited by Jakob Merlo-Horstius. Cologne: Petri Henningii, 1631.

Evagrius Ponticus. *Evagrius Ponticus: Praktikos and Chapters on Prayer.* Edited by J. E. Bamberger. Cistercian Studies Series 4. Spencer: Spencer, 1970.

Evans, Robert. *Reception History, Tradition and Biblical Interpretation: Gadamer and Jauss in Current Practice.* London: Bloomsbury, 2014.

Fairbairn, Donald. "Patristic Exegesis and Theology: The Cart and the Horse." *WTJ* 69 (2007) 1-19.

Fee, Gordon D. *The First and Second Letters to the Thessalonians.* NICNT. Edited by Gordon D. Fee. Grand Rapids: Eerdmans, 2009.

Field, Frederick, ed. *Ioannis Chrysostomi interpretatio omnium epistularum Paulinarum.* 7 vols. Oxford: J. H. Parker, 1854-62.

Foster, Paul. "Who Wrote 2 Thessalonians? A Fresh Look at an Old Problem." *JSNT* 35.2 (2012) 150-75.

Fransen, Paul-Irénée. "Description de la collection grégorienne de Florus de Lyons sur l'apôtre." *RBén* 98 (1988) 278-317.

———. "Description de la collection hiéronymienne de Florus de Lyons sur l'apôtre." *RBén* 94 (1984) 195-228.

Gamble, Richard C. "Calvin as Theologian and Exegete: Is There Anything New?" In *The Organizational Structure of Calvin's Theology*, edited by Richard C. Gamble, 44-60. New York/London: Garland, 1992.

Ganoczy, Alexandre, and Klaus Müller. *Calvins Handschriftliche Annotationen zu Chrysostomus: Ein Beitrag zur Hermeneutik Calvins.* Wiesbaden: Steiner, 1981.

Gilmont, Jean-Francois. *John Calvin and the Printed Book.* Translated by Karin Maag. Kirksville: Truman State University Press, 2005.

Goering, Joseph W. "An Introduction to Medieval Christian Biblical Interpretation." In *With Reverence for the Word*, edited by Jan McAuliffe, et al., 197-203. Oxford: Oxford University Press, 2003.

BIBLIOGRAPHY

Goez, Werner. "Simonie." *RGG* 7:1328–29.

González, Justo L. *The Story of Christianity*. Vol. 2. San Francisco: Harper & Row, 1984.

Goodrich, Richard J. *Contextualizing Cassian: Aristocrats, Asceticism, and Reformation in Fifth-Century Gaul*. Oxford: Oxford University Press, 2007.

Greef, Wulfert de. "Calvin's Writings." In *The Cambridge Companion to John Calvin*, edited by Donald K. McKim, 41–57. Cambridge: Cambridge University Press, 2004.

———. *The Writings of John Calvin: An Introductory Guide*. Leicester: Apollos, 1993.

Green, Joel B. *Seized by Truth: Reading the Bible as Scripture*. Nashville: Abingdon, 2007.

Gregory the Great. *The Letters of Gregory the Great*. Translated by John R. C Martyn. Toronto: Pontifical Institute of Mediaeval Studies, 2004.

Haimo of Auxerre. "Exposition of the Second Letter to the Thessalonians." In *Second Thessalonians: Two Early Medieval Apocalyptic Commentaries*, edited and translated by Kevin L. Hughes, 13–33. Kalamazoo: Medieval Institute, 2001.

Hall, Basil. "Calvin and Biblical Humanism." In *Influences upon Calvin and Discussion of the 1559 Institutes*, edited by Richard C. Gamble, 55–69. Vol. 4 of *Articles on Calvin and Calvinism*. New York and London: Garland, 1992.

Harbison, E. Harris. "History and Destiny." *ThTo* 21.4 (1965) 395–409.

Hart, David Bentley. *The Beauty of the Infinite: The Aesthetics of Christian Truth*. Grand Rapids: Eerdmans, 2004.

Hartney, Aideen M. *John Chrysostom and the Transformation of the City*. London: Duckworth, 2004.

Hazlett, W. Ian P. "Calvin's Latin Preface to His Proposed French Edition of Chrysostom's Homilies: Translation and Commentary." In *Humanism and Reform: The Church in Europe, England, and Scotland, 1400-1643*, edited by James Kirk, 129–50. Vol. 8 of *Studies in Church History*. Oxford: Blackwell, 1991.

Heil, Johannes. "Haimo's Commentary on Paul: Sources, Methods and Theology." In *Études d'exégèse carolingienne autour d'Haymon d'Auxerre*, edited by Sumi Shimahara, 103–22. Collection Haut Moyen Âge 4. Turnhout: Brepols, 2007.

———. *Kompilation oder Konstruktion? Die Juden in den Pauluskommentaren des 9. Jahrhunderts*. Forschungen zur Geschichte der Juden 6. Hannover: Hahnsche, 1998.

———. "Labourers in the Lord's Quarry: Carolingian Exegetes, Patristic Authority, and Theological Innovation, a Case Study in the Representation of Jews in the Commentaries on Paul." In *The Study of the Bible in the Carolingian Era*, edited by Celia Chazelle and Burton van Name Edwards, 75–96. Turnhout: Brepols, 2003.

———. "Theodulf, Haimo, and Jewish Traditions of Biblical Learning: Exploring Carolingian Culture's Lost Spanish Heritage." In *Discovery and Distinction in the Early Middle Ages: Studies in Honor of John J. Contreni*, edited by Cullen J. Chandler and Steven Stofferahn, 103–34. Kalamazoo: Medieval Institute, 2013.

Hill, Joyce. "Carolingian Perspectives on the Authority of Bede." In *Innovation and Tradition in the Writings of the Venerable Bede*, edited by Scott DeGregorio, 227–49. Morgantown: West Virginia University Press, 2006.

Hirsch, Eric D. *Validity in Interpretation*. London: Yale University Press, 1967.

Holder, R. Ward. "Calvin as Commentator on the Pauline Epistles." In *Calvin and the Bible*, edited by Donald K. McKim, 224–56. Cambridge: Cambridge University Press, 2006.

———. "*Ecclesia, legenda atque intelligenda scriptura*: The Church as Discerning Community in Calvin's Hermeneutics." *CTJ* 36.2 (2001) 270–89.

Bibliography

Holwerda, David E. "Eschatology and History: A Look at Calvin's Eschatological Vision." In *Calvin's Theology, Theology Proper, Eschatology*, edited by Richard C. Gamble, 130–59. Vol. 9 of *Articles on Calvin and Calvinism*. New York: Garland, 1992.

Hughes, Kevin L. "Augustine and Adversary: Strategies of Synthesis in Early Medieval Exegesis." In *History, Apocalypse, and the Secular Imagination: New Essays on Augustine's City of God*, edited by Mark Vessey, et al., 221–33. Augustinian Studies. Bowling Green: Philosophy Documentation Center, 1999.

———. *Constructing Antichrist*. Washington, DC: Catholic University of America Press, 2005.

———. "Haimo of Auxerre and the Fruition of Carolingian Hermeneutics." In *Second Thessalonians: Two Early Medieval Apocalyptic Commentaries*, edited by E. Ann Matter, 13–20. Kalamazoo: Medieval Institute, 2001.

Iogna-Prat, Dominique. "L'œuvre d'Haymon d'Auxerre: état de la question." In *L'École carolingienne d'Auxerre: de Murethach à Rémi, 830–908*, edited by Dominique Iogna-Prat, et al., 157–79. Paris: Beauchesne, 1991.

Iser, Wolfgang. *Prospecting: From Reader Response to Literary Anthropology*. London: Johns Hopkins University Press, 1993.

Isidore of Seville. *The Etymologies*. Translated by Stephen A Barney, Jennifer A. Beach, Oliver Berghof, and W. J. Lewis. Cambridge: Cambridge University Press, 2002.

Janz, Denis R. *A Reformation Reader*. Minneapolis: Fortress, 1990.

Jauss, Hans-Robert. *Aesthetic Experience and Literary Hermeneutics*. Translated by Michael Shaw. Edited by Wlad Godzich and Jochen Schulte-Sasse. Theory and History of Literature 3. Minneapolis: University of Minnesota Press, 1982.

———. "The Alterity and Modernity of Medieval Literature." *New Literary History*. 10.2 (1979) 181–229.

———. "Literaturgeschichte als Provokation der Literaturwissenschaft." In *Rezeptionsästhetik. Uni-Taschenbücher*, edited by Rainer Warning, 126–62. München: Willhelm Fink Verlag, 1979.

———. *Question and Answer: Forms of Dialogic Understanding*. Translated by Michael Hays. Edited by Wlad Godzich and Jochen Schulte-Sasse. Theory and History of Literature 68. Minneapolis: University of Minnesota Press, 1989.

———. "The Theory of Reception: A Retrospective of Its Unrecognized Prehistory." In *Literary Theory Today*, edited by Peter Collier and Helga Geyer-Ryan, 53–73. Ithaca: Cornell University Press, 1992.

———. *Toward an Aesthetic of Reception*. Translated by Timothy Bahti. Edited by Wlad Godzich and Jochen Schulte-Sasse. Theory and History of Literature 2. Minneapolis: University of Minnesota Press, 1982.

———. "Tradition, Innovation, and Aesthetic Experience." *Journal of Aesthetics and Art Criticism* 46.3 (1988) 375–88.

Kelly, J. N. D. *Early Christian Doctrines*. 5th rev. ed. London: Continuum, 2001.

———. *Golden Mouth*. London: Duckworth, 1995.

King, Jonathan. *The Beauty of the Lord: Theology As Aesthetics*. Bellingham: Lexham, 2018.

Kosík, Karel. *Dialectics of the Concrete: A Study on Problems of Man and World*. Dordrecht: D. Reidel, 1976.

Kovacs, Judith, and Christopher Rowland. *Revelation: The Apocalypse of Jesus Christ*. Blackwell Bible Commentaries. Oxford: Blackwell, 2004.

Kristeller, Paul Oskar. *Renaissance Thought and Its Sources*. New York: Columbia University Press, 1979.

BIBLIOGRAPHY

Landes, Richard. "The Fear of an Apocalyptic Year 1000: Augustinian Historiography, Medieval and Modern." *Speculum* 75.1 (2000) 91–145.

———. "Lest the Millennium Be Fulfilled: Apocalyptic Expectations and the Pattern of Western Chronography 100–800 CE." In *The Use and Abuse of Eschatology in the Middle Ages*, edited by Werner Verbeke, et al., 137–211. Leuven: Leuven University Press, 1988.

Lane, Anthony N.S. *John Calvin: Student of the Church Fathers*. Edinburgh: T. & T. Clark, 1999.

Liebeschuetz, J. H. W. G. *Antioch: City and Imperial Administration in the Later Roman Empire*. Oxford: Oxford University Press, 1972.

———. *Barbarians and Bishops: Army, Church, and State in the Age of Arcadius and Chrysostom*. Oxford: Oxford University Press, 1990.

Lindberg, Carter. *A Brief History of Christianity*. Oxford: Blackwell, 2006.

Little, Lester K. "Calvin's Appreciation of Gregory the Great." *HTR* 56.2 (1963) 145–57.

Lobrichon, Guy. "Stalking the Signs: The Apocalyptic Commentaries." In *The Apocalyptic Year 1000: Religious Expectation and Social Change, 950–1050*, edited by Richard Landes, et al., 67–80. Oxford: Oxford University Press, 2003.

Luther, Martin. *D. Martin Luthers Werke*. Kritische Gesamtausgabe. 73 vols. Weimar: Herman Böhlaus, 1883–2009.

———. *Luther's Works*. Edited by Jaroslav Pelikan and Helmut T. Lehman. 75 vols. Philadelphia: Muehlenberg/Fortress; St. Louis: Concordia, 1955–86.

Lynch, Joseph H. *Simoniacal Entry into Religious Life from 1000 to 1260*. Columbus: Ohio State University Press, 1976.

Malherbe, Abraham. *The Letters to the Thessalonians*. Vol. 32B of *The Anchor Bible*. Edited by David Noel Freedman. New York: Doubleday, 2000.

Maloney, George A. *Pseudo-Macarius*. The Classics of Western Spirituality. New York: Paulist, 1992.

Markus, R. A. *Gregory the Great and His World*. Cambridge: Cambridge University Press, 1997.

Marshall, I. Howard. *1 and 2 Thessalonians*. New Century Bible Commentary. Grand Rapids: Eerdmans, 1983.

Matter, E. Ann. "Haimo's Commentary on the Song of Songs and the Traditions of the Carolingian Schools." In *Études d'exégèse carolingienne autour d'Haymon d'Auxerre*, edited by Sumi Shimahara, 89–101. Collection Haut Moyen Âge 4. Turnhout: Brepols, 2007.

Mayer, Wendy. *The Homilies of St. John Chrysostom–Provenance*. OrChrAn 273. Rome: Pontifica Istituto Orientalo, 2005.

———. "Poverty and Generosity in the Time of Chrysostom." In *Wealth and Poverty in Early Church and Society*, edited by Susan R. Holman, 140–58. Grand Rapids: Baker Academic, 2008.

Mayer, Wendy, and Pauline Allen. *John Chrysostom*. Edited by Carol Harrison. Early Church Fathers. London: Routledge, 2000.

McEvoy, J. J. *Robert Grosseteste*. Oxford: Oxford University Press, 2000.

McGinn, Bernard. *Antichrist: Two Thousand Years of the Human Fascination with Evil*. San Francisco: Harper, 1994.

Mealand, David. "The Extent of the Pauline Corpus: A Multivariate Approach." *JSNT* 18.59 (1995) 61–92.

Bibliography

Mégier, Elisabeth. "Jewish Converts in the Early Church and Latin Christian Exegetes of Isaiah, c. 400–1150." *JEH* 59.1 (2008) 1–28.
Melanchthon, Philip. *De ecclesia et de auctoritate verbi dei*. Edited by Robert Stupperich. Vol. 1 of *Melanchthons Werke*. Gütersloh: C. Bertelsmann, 1951.
Migne, J.-P., ed. *Patrologia graeca*. 162 vols. Paris: J.-P. Migne, 1857–86.
———. *Patrologia latina*. 217 vols. Paris: J.-P. Migne, 1844–64.
Mitchell, Margaret. *The Heavenly Trumpet*. London: Westminster John Knox, 2002.
Murethach. *In Donati artem maiorem*. Edited by Louis Holtz. CCCM 40. Turnhout: Brepols, 1977.
Nancy, Jean-Luc. *The Sense of the World*. Minneapolis: University of Minnesota Press, 1997.
Nassif, Bradley. "Theōria." In *Encyclopedia of Early Christianity*, edited by Everett Ferguson, et al., 1122–23. New York: Routledge, 1999.
Nicholas de Lyra. *Glossa Ordinaria*. Vol. 6. Venice: Paganinus di Paganinis, 1603.
O'Brien, Peter Thomas. *Introductory Thanksgivings in the Letters of Paul*. Vol. 49 of NovTSup. Leiden: Brill, 1977.
———. "Thanksgiving and the Gospel in Paul." *New Testam. Stud.* 21 (1975) 144–55.
O'Loughlin, T. "*Res, tempus, locus, persona*: Adomnán's Exegetical Method." In *Spes Scotorum Hope of Scots*, edited by Dauvit Broun and Thomas Owen Clancy, 139–58. Edinburgh: T. & T. Clark, 1999.
Osborn, Eric F. "Love." *Encyclopedia of Early Christianity*, edited by Everett Ferguson, et al., 693–97. New York: Routledge, 1999.
Osborne, Grant R. *The Hermeneutical Spiral*. 2nd ed. Downers Grove, IL: InterVarsity, 2006.
Otten, Willemien. "Carolingian Theology." In *The Medieval Theologians*, edited by G. R. Evans, 65–82. Oxford: Blackwell, 2001.
Ozment, Steven. *The Age of Reform, 1250–1550*. New Haven: Yale University Press, 1980.
Paddison, Angus. "The Authority of Scripture and the Triune God." *IJST* 13.4 (2011) 448–62.
Pannenberg, Wolfhart. *Basic Questions in Theology*. Edited by George H. Kehm. Translated by Paul J. Achtemeier. Vol. 1. Philadelphia: Fortress, 1970.
Parker, T. H. L. *Calvin's New Testament Commentaries*. London: SCM, 1971.
———. *John Calvin: A Biography*. London: J. M. Dent & Sons, 1975.
Parris, David Paul. *Reception Theory and Biblical Hermeneutics*. Eugene, OR: Pickwick, 2009.
Paul of Bernried. "The Life of Gregory VII." In *The Papal Reform of the Eleventh Century: Lives of Pope Leo IX and Pope Gregory VII*, edited and translated by Ian Stuart Robinson, 262–365. Manchester: Manchester University Press, 2004.
Pelagius. *Exposito in ii Thessalonicenses*. Vol. 9 of *Pelagius's Expositions of Thirteen Epistles of St. Paul*. Edited by J. Armitage Robinson. Cambridge: Cambridge University Press, 1926.
Pelikan, Jaroslav. *Divine Rhetoric: The Sermon on the Mount As Message and As Model in Augustine, Chrysostom, and Luther*. Crestwood: St. Vladimir's Seminary Press, 2000.
———. *The Growth of Medieval Theology (600–1300)*. Vol. 3 of *The Christian Tradition*. Chicago: The University of Chicago Press, 1978.
———. *Reformation of Church and Dogma (1300–1700)*. Vol. 4 of *The Christian Tradition*. Chicago: University of Chicago Press, 1983.

Bibliography

Placher, William C. *The Domestication of Transcendence: How Modern Thinking about God Went Wrong.* Louisville: Westminster John Knox, 1996.
Quadri, Riccardo. "Aimone di Auxerre alla luce dei 'Collectanea' di Heiric di Auxerre." *Italia Medioevale e Umanistica* 6 (1963) 1–48.
Quistorp, Heinrich. *Calvin's Doctrine of the Last Things.* Translated by Harold Knight. London: Lutterworth, 1955.
Rae, Murray. "Biblical Theology and the Communicative Presence of God." In *The Bible as Christian Scripture: The Work of Brevard S. Childs,* edited by Christopher R. Seitz and Kent H. Richards, 137–54. Atlanta: SBL, 2013.
Ratzinger, Joseph. *Introduction to Christianity.* San Francisco: Ignatius, 2004.
Riddlebarger, Kim. *The Man of Sin: Uncovering the Truth About the Antichrist.* Grand Rapids: Baker, 2006.
Rigaux, Beda. *Saint Paul: Les épitres aux Thessaloniciens.* Études Bibliques. Paris: Gabalda, 1956.
Riggenbach, Eduard. *Die ältesten lateinischen Kommentare zum Hebräerbrief.* Leipzig: A. Deichert, 1907.
Roberts, Alexander, and James Donaldson, eds. *The Ante-Nicene Fathers.* 10 vols. Peabody: Hendrickson, 1885.
Rusch, Adolph. *Biblia cum Glossa Ordinaria: Facsimile Reprints of the Editio Princeps Adolph Rusch of Strausburg 1480/81.* Vol. 4. Turnhout: Brepols, 1992.
Rush, Ormond. *The Reception of Doctrine.* Edited by Gerald O'Collins and Jared Wicks. Serie Teologia. Rome: Gregorian University Press, 1997.
Schaff, Philip, ed. *The Nicene and Post-Nicene Fathers.* Series 1. 14 vols. Peabody: Hendrickson, 1886.
———. *The Nicene and Post-Nicene Fathers.* Series 2. 14 vols. Peabody: Hendrickson, 1886.
Severian von Gabala. "Fragmenta in epistulam ii ad Thessalonicenses." In *Pauluskommentare aus der griechischen Kirche,* edited by Karl Staab, 332–36. Munich: Aschendorffschen, 1933.
Smalley, Beryl. *The Study of the Bible in the Middle Ages.* Oxford: Blackwell, 1952.
Steinmetz, David C. "Calvin and the Patristic Exegesis of Paul." In *The Bible in the Sixteenth Century,* edited by David C. Steinmetz, 100–118. Durham: Duke University Press, 1990.
———. *Calvin in Context.* New York: Oxford University Press, 1995.
Sterk, Andrea. *Renouncing the World Yet Leading the Church: The Monk-Bishop in Late Antiquity.* Cambridge: Harvard University Press, 2004.
Swanson, Jenny. "The Glossa Ordinaria." In *The Medieval Theologians,* edited by G. R. Evans, 156–67. Oxford: Blackwell, 2001.
Theodore of Mopsuestia. "In epistolam B. Pauli ii Thessalonicenses." In *In epistolas B. Pauli commentarii,* edited by H. B. Swete, 1–40. Cambridge: Cambridge University Press, 1880.
Theodoret of Cyrus. "The Second Letter to the Thessalonians." In *Commentary on the Letters of Saint Paul,* edited and translated by Robert Charles Hill, 125–35. Brookline: Holy Cross Orthodox, 2001.
Thietland of Einselden. "In epistolam ii ad Thessalonicenses." In *Second Thessalonians: Two Early Medieval Apocalyptic Commentaries,* edited and translated by Steven R. Cartwright, 35–76. Kalamazoo: Medieval Institute, 2001.

Bibliography

Thiselton, Anthony C. *1 and 2 Thessalonians Through the Centuries*. Edited by Judith Kovacs. Blackwell Bible Commentaries. Oxford: Blackwell, 2010.
———. *The First Epistle to the Corinthians*. NIGTC. Edited by I. Howard Marshall and Donald Hagner. Grand Rapids: Eerdmans, 2000.
———. *Hermeneutics: An Introduction*. Cambridge: Eerdmans, 2009.
———. *The Hermeneutics of Doctrine*. Grand Rapids: Eerdmans, 2007.
———. *New Horizons in Hermeneutics*. Grand Rapids: Zondervan, 1992.
Thomas Aquinas. *Summa Theologiae*. New York: Catholic Way, 2014.
Thompson, John L. "Calvin as a Biblical Interpreter." In *The Cambridge Companion to John Calvin*, edited by Donald K. McKim, 58–73. Cambridge: Cambridge University Press, 2004.
Thomson, John A. F. *The Western Church in the Middle Ages*. London: Arnold, 1998.
Torrance, T. F. *The Hermeneutics of John Calvin*. Edinburgh: Scottish Academic, 1988.
Wakefield, Walter L., and Austin P. Evans, eds. *Heresies of the High Middle Ages: Selected Sources*. Translated by Walter L. Wakefield and Austin P. Evans. New York: Columbia University Press, 1991.
Walchenbach, John R. *John Calvin as Biblical Commentator: An Investigation into Calvin's Use of John Chrysostom as an Exegetical Tutor*. Eugene, OR: Wipf & Stock, 2010.
Wallace-Hadrill, D. S. *Christian Antioch*. Cambridge: Cambridge University Press, 1982.
Wanamaker, Charles A. *The Epistles to the Thessalonians*. NIGTC. Edited by I. Howard Marshall and W. Ward Gasque. Grand Rapids: Eerdmans, 1990.
Wannenwetsch, Bernd. "Conversing with the Saints as They Converse with Scripture." *EuroJTh* 18.2 (2009) 125–36.
Warfield, Benjamin B. *Calvin and Augustine*. Philadelphia: Presbyterian and Reformed, 1956.
Wendel, Francois. *Calvin: The Origins and Development of His Religious Thought*. Translated by Philip Mairet. London: Collins, 1976.
Wessel, Susan. *Cyril of Alexandria and the Nestorian Controversy: The Making of a Saint and of a Heretic*. Oxford: Oxford University Press, 2004.
Wilder, Terry L. *Pseudonymity, the New Testament, and Deception: An Inquiry into Intention and Reception*. Lanham: University Press of America, 2004.
Wilken, Robert Louis. "*In novissimis diebus*: Biblical Promises, Jewish Hopes, and Early Christian Exegesis." In *Norms of Faith and Life*, edited by E. Ferguson, 139–57. New York: Garland, 1999.
Witherington, Ben, III. *1 and 2 Thessalonians: A Socio-Rhetorical Commentary*. Grand Rapids: Eerdmans, 2006.
Young, Frances M. *Biblical Exegesis and the Formation of Christian Culture*. Cambridge: Cambridge University Press, 1997.
Zaharopoulos, Dimitri Z. *Theodore of Mopsuestia on the Bible*. New York: Paulist, 1989.
Zwingli, Ulrich. "In ii. epistolam ad Thessalonicenses annotationes." In *Huldrici Zuinglii opera*, edited by Melchiore Schulero and Io. Schultessio, 239–48. Vol. 6. Zürich: Schultessiana, 1836.

Subject Index

Acts of Peter and Paul, 62–63
Admonán, 10
Adso of Montier-en-Der, 52
Ælfric of Eynsham, 52
aesthetic experience, 9–12, 92
Alcuin of York, 51, 79
Alighieri, Dante, 62, 115, 129
Allen, Pauline, 18–27
almsgiving, 19, 38–39
Altaner, Berthold, 31
Ambrose of Milan, 41, 56–57
Ambrosiaster, 56, 58, 65–68, 72, 75–79, 111, 118
anabaptists, 95, 118
Anderson, Gary A., 44
Antiochus Epiphanes, 48
Apocalypse of Daniel, 1
apocalyptic realism, 53, 58, 65, 72
Aristotle, 11, 124
asceticism, 19, 22–23, 26–30, 38–39, 42–49
Augustine, 20, 29, 31–32, 43, 47, 52, 55–59, 64–65, 70–79, 82–85, 102, 111–12, 115–16

Backus, Irena, 43–44
Barré, Henri, 53
Barth, Karl, 98–99
Basil of Caesarea, 29, 35, 39–40, 45–46
Baum, Armin D., 5
Bavinck, Herman, 12–13
Beauty, beautiful, 9–16, 109, 124–127
Bede, 51–52, 55–56, 70–71, 114
Beker, J. C., 5
Bell, Richard, ix, 44

Berengar of Tours, 82, 113–14
Berthelier, Philibert, 94
Best, Ernest, 32, 37, 96, 109
Biondo, Flavio, 113
Bockmuehl, Markus, 2
Bonaventure, 52, 75, 78
Boniface VIII, Pope, 82, 115
Bornemann, Wilhelm, 75
Boucaud, Pierre, 74
Boussett, Wilhelm, 63
Brandes, Wolfram, 70
Brändle, Rudolf, 18–19, 39
bride-chamber, 34
Bright, Pamela, 43
Bruno the Carthusian, 111, 116
Bucer, Martin, 83
Bullinger, Heinrich, 103
Burgess, Richard, 70
Burkitt, F., 43

Cajetan, 82, 89, 91, 96, 116
Caligula, 48
Calvin, John, 1, 3–4, 20, 35, 41–42, 47, 60, 81–127
Candler, Peter, 15–17, 123
Cartwright, Steven, 70
Casiday, A., 46
Cassiodor, 56
Charlemagne, 67, 70
Charlesworth, James, 1, 44
Chase, 20, 23, 25, 45
chiliasm, 70–71, 79, 108
Clarke, W. K. Lowther, 39, 45
Claudius of Turin, 52
Clement of Alexandria, 29, 69

Subject Index

Colish, Marcia, 50, 64–65
Communion, 61, 85, 94–95, 103
Contreni, John J., 51, 56, 58, 64
Cooper, Kate, 31
Corrigan, Kevin, 46
Cottret, Bernard, 92
Cyprian of Carthage, 29, 56
Cyril of Alexandria, 24, 63
Cyril of Jerusalem, 138

Diocletian, 54, 64, 68
Diodore of Tarsus, 19, 22–26, 45
Dowey, Edward, 86
Dudden, F., 61

ecclesiology, 1, 4, 86, 97, 102–5
Eldridge, Michael, 44
Elliott, Mark, 7, 12
Elizabeth I, 95
Ephrem the Syrian, 34, 56
Erasmus, Desiderius, 82–83, 115
Eriugena, John Scottus, 51
eschatology, 4–5, 15, 27, 33–37, 42–45, 49, 54, 57, 70–73, 79, 85, 90–91, 97, 105–10, 113, 116, 119–123, 126
Estius, 82, 89–91, 96, 116
Eusebius of Caesarea, 64, 70
Evagrius Ponticus, 20, 39–40, 45–46
Evans, Robert, 4, 10
Evans, Austin, 63
excommunication, 85, 92–97, 105

Fairbairn, Donald, 23
Fee, Gordon, 32, 37
florilegia, 52
Florus of Lyon, 52, 56
Foster, Paul, 5
Fransen, Paul-Irénée, 56

Gadamer, Hans Georg, 4, 8
Gamble, Richard, 97
Ganoczy, Alexandre, 83
Georgius of Sicily, 100
Gilmont, Jean-Francois, 83
Glossa Ordinaria, 20, 37, 51–52, 56, 78
Goez, Werner, 61
González, Justo, 115

Goodrich, Richard, 46
Gottschalk of Orbais, 58–60
Greef, Wulfert de, 84, 94
Green, Joel, x, 95–96,
Gregory VII, 63–64
Gregory of Nyssa, 45
Gregory the Great, 56–58, 61, 67–68, 76, 113, 117, 119
Grosseteste, Robert, 120

Haddington, John Major, 86
Hall, Basil, 121
Harbison, E., 107
Hart, David Bently, 11–12, 16, 126
Hartney, Aideen, 19, 22
Haymo of Halberstadt, 50
Hazlett, W., 83
Heil, Johannes, xi, 50–51, 56, 74, 77
Heiric of Auxerre, 52
Henry IV, 63
heresy, heretics, 58, 61–65, 78–79, 89, 111, 123, 125
Hesshusen, Tilemann, 103
Hilary of Poitiers, 56
Hincmar of Reims, 58–60
Hippolytus, 69–70, 73, 76–78
Hirsch, E. D., 2
Holder, R., 83–84, 87
Holtz, Louis, 51
Holy Spirit, 7, 62–63, 76, 84, 103, 105, 117, 121
Holwerda, David, 106–10, 113, 119
horizon of expectation, 3, 9–11, 20, 23, 28, 32, 35, 49, 57, 64, 67, 71, 89, 96, 122, 125
Hubmaier, Balthasar, 95
Hughes, Kevin L., 4, 24, 40, 51, 53, 56–57, 66, 68, 70, 72, 74–76, 111, 113, 116
Hus, Jan, 111, 119–20
humanism, 81, 86, 121, 125

idle, 38–42, 55, 84, 93, 104
Innocent III, Pope, 111
investiture, 62, 64, 79
Iogna-Prat, Dominique, 52
Institutes of the Christian Religion, 4, 69, 82–88, 93–94, 98–116, 121

Irenaeus of Lyon, 20, 34, 42, 63–64
Iser, Wolfgang, 8
Isidore of Seville, 74–75
Islam, 111, 119

Janz, Denis, 95
Jauss, Hans Robert, ix, 2–17, 20, 38, 79, 92, 125–26
Jerome, 52, 56–58, 61, 66–68, 70, 75–79, 116
Jews, Judaism, 47, 65, 76–78, 118
John Cassian, 20, 29, 39, 40–41, 46–47, 56–57
John of Damascus, 20, 28, 37, 41
John of Constantinople, 113
Julian of Eclanum, 31
Julian the Apostate, 31, 54, 64, 68
Justin Martyr, 63

Kelly, J. N. D., 18–27
Kosík, Karel, 8
Kovacs, Judith, 53
Kristeller, Paul, 81

Lactantius, 69
Landes, Richard, 67, 69–71
Lane, Anthony, 86
Leo I (the Great), Pope, 36, 113
Leo III, Pope, 70
Leo X, Pope, 115
Liebeschuetz, J. H. W. G., 19–20, 22
Lindberg, Carter, 62
Lobrichon, Guy, 71
Lombard, Peter, 52, 64–66, 72, 113
Lucian of Antioch, 23
Lupus, Servatus, 58
Luther, Martin, 1, 62, 90–91, 94–96, 99, 103, 106, 109, 116–120, 125
Lynch, Joseph, 62

Machiavelli, 113
Malherbe, Abraham, 97
Maloney, George, 45
man of lawlessness, man of sin, 38, 42, 48, 54, 57, 68, 73, 75, 85, 114, 117–18, 123,
Markus, R., 61
Marshall, I. H., 109

Mass, 117–119, 125
Matter, E. Ann, 51
Maurus, Rabanus, 51, 57–58, 72, 76
Mayer, Wendy, ix, 18–27, 39
McGinn, Bernard, 43, 63, 111, 120
McEvoy, J., 120
Mealand, David, 5
Mégier, Elisabeth, 77
Melanchthon, Philip, 82–83, 113
Meletius of Antioch, 18–19
Methodius, 36
Michael (archangel), 54, 67–68, 71, 76
millenarianism, 58, 69–70, 79
millennium, 43, 68–73
Mitchell, Margaret, 25–26, 28
Müller, Klaus, 83
Murethach, 51–52
mystery of iniquity, 54, 64, 68, 72, 74–76, 111–12, 116, 120

Nancy, Jean-Luc, 2
Nero, 54, 62, 64, 68, 72
Nestorius, 23
Nicholas III, Pope, 62
Nicholas de Lyra, 37

O'Brien, Peter, 28
O'Loughlin, Thomas, ix, 52
Origen of Alexandria, 20, 24, 44, 56, 63
Orosius, 70
Ortigues, 55
Osborn, Eric, 29
Osborne, Grant, 2
Otten, Willemien, 59
Ozment, Steven, 94

Paddison, Angus, 6
Pannenberg, Wolfhart, 11
papacy, 1, 62–63, 85–87, 94, 96, 102, 110, 112, 114–120, 124
Parker, T., 81–83
Parris, David, 3, 10, 12
Paul of Bernried, 63
Pelagius, 71, 75
Pelikan, Jaroslav, 18, 25, 59–60, 108, 111, 115, 118
Placher, William, 86, 109
Polycarp of Smyrna, 34, 36

Subject Index

poor, 19, 27, 30, 38-42, 53, 64, 85, 96
positivism, 4, 9, 12, 15, 23, 126
predestination, 57-60, 63, 79, 86-87, 100-2, 123
pride, 23, 27, 30, 33, 36, 38-49, 119
Prosper, 57, 59
Pseudo-Hippolytus, 45, 63
Pseudo-Macarius, 45-46
pseudonymity, 5, 84, 101

Quadri, 51, 58
Quistorp, 106-7, 109

Radbertus, Paschasius, 52
Rae, Murray, x, 7
Ratzinger, Joseph, 15
reception history, 3-4, 7-8, 10, 13-4, 16, 60, 76, 79, 83, 96, 105, 112, 121, 123-25
Remigius of Auxerre, 50, 52
Rezeptionsästhetik, 2-17, 71, 123-25
rhetoric, 18, 21-26, 30-32, 35-37, 42, 49, 81, 86-87, 90, 123, 126
Riddlebarger, Kim, 114
Rigaux, Beda, 32, 37, 48-49
Riggenbach, Eduard, 50-51, 58
Roman Empire, Rome, 54, 66, 68-72, 74, 76, 78-79, 85, 110, 112-13, 116
Rowland, Christopher, x, 53
Rule of St. Benedict, 55
Rusch Glossa, 52
Rush, Ormond, ix, 7, 9-15

Satan, 13, 33, 42-46, 48-49, 54, 68, 73-74, 99-102, 112, 114-15, 119
Schubert, Paul, 28
Scottus, Sedulius, 57, 72, 75
Scotus, John Duns, 86, 98
Severian of Gabala, 20, 33-34, 47
Signorelli, Luca, 74
Simon Magus (simony), 54, 58, 60-65, 75, 79, 105, 115, 123, 125
sloth, 30, 36
Smalley, Beryl, 51
Smaragdus of Saint-Mihiel, 52, 55
Socrates Scholasticus, 47

speech-acts, 6
Steinmetz, David, 83, 86, 101
Sterk, Andrea, 19, 39
Swanson, Jenny, 51
Synod of Mainz, 58
Synod of Oak, 20

Tertullian, 44, 76
Theodore of Mopsuestia, 18, 20, 23-24, 28, 31-34, 37, 40-41, 44, 46, 57, 71
Theodoret of Cyrus, 20, 24, 28, 31-34, 37, 44
Theodulf of Orléans, 51, 74
Theophilus of Antioch, 69
Theophylact, 20
Theoria, 23-25
Thietland of Einsiedeln, 37, 53, 70-71
Thiselton, Anthony, ix, 6, 8, 10-11, 28, 31, 34, 73, 75, 90
Thomas á Kempis, 82, 108
Thomas Aquinas, 7, 52, 60, 75
Thompson, John L., 83, 86
Thomson, John A., 62
Torrance, T. F., 86, 108
tradition, 8, 10, 14, 20, 23-24, 37, 42, 44, 46, 48-51, 56-60, 63-66, 72, 75-76, 79-80, 102, 108-111, 115-20
transubstantiation, 64, 103
Trilling, Wolfgang, 5
Trinity, trinitarianism, 6, 15-16, 19, 126
Tyconian-Augustine interpretation, 53, 110, 116, 121
Tyconius, 20, 43, 53

vice, 27, 43-49, 73, 123
Vincentian canon, 56
virtue, 27-35, 42, 45-49, 55, 58, 82, 123-24

Wakefield, Walter, 63
Walchenbach, John, 47, 83, 86
Wanamaker, Charles, 37, 48-49, 96
Wannewetsch, Bernd, 6
Warfield, Benjamin, 102

Wendel, Francois, 98
Westminster Confession of Faith, 125
Wilder, Terry L., 5
Wilken, Robert, 21–22
William of Occam, 86
Wrede, William, 5

Wyclif, 111, 120

Young, Frances, 21, 24

Zwingli, Ulrich, 82, 89–92, 95–96, 103, 117